Earle S Hotta was a counselor/educator for 41 years in Hawaii Public Schools and Colleges, but also in Brazil as a peace corps volunteer and teacher at the American School of Recife. He was born and raised on the island of Maui when it was still a territory and comes from a family who immigrated from Hiroshima, Japan, during the Meiji Period (1868–1912).

His introduction and passion for people began with parents who surrounded their home with guests from movie stars to wood carvers and professional baseball players as well as people they befriended at their shop.

To Ms. Carolina whose advice I listen to 98%, no, make that 97.5% of the time.

And

Don Frederico who always encouraged me to write.

Earle S Hotta

THE RICE TREE CHRONICLES

AUSTIN MACAULEY PUBLISHERS™

LONDON • CAMBRIDGE • NEW YORK • SHARJAH

Ordering Information
Quantity sales: Special discounts are available on quantity purchases by corporations, associations, and others. For details, contact the publisher at the address below.

Publisher's Cataloging-in-Publication data
Hotta, Earle S
The Rice Tree Chronicles

ISBN 9781649798107 (Paperback)
ISBN 9781649798114 (ePub e-book)

Library of Congress Control Number: 2023919192

www.austinmacauley.com/us

First Published 2024
Austin Macauley Publishers LLC
40 Wall Street, 33rd Floor, Suite 3302
New York, NY 10005
USA

mail-usa@austinmacauley.com
+1 (646) 5125767

To the many teachers, friends and people who shared their lives as well as stories with me.

Along the River of Dawn

The Chao Phraya has many names, the River of Dawn being but one is without a doubt the most famous of all waterways in Thailand. It runs over 231 miles and its tributaries reach all corners of the country and its waters feed millions of hectares of rice. The stories along the River of Dawn center around its most famous hub, the city of Bangkok.

Bangkok Confidential

There is a certain Starbucks with a single bar facing a large picture window fronting a sidewalk on Sukumvit Road in Bangkok. The "people watching" is one of the best that I have encountered here considering that I had been recently glued to poor choices of reality TV shows at home.

Sitting next to me are three young visitors from New York enjoying the live-action dramas being played out before our eyes. Ladyboys or "Katoy" are openly soliciting business in the streets.

They stand in the shadows of the night or in the shade of midday, all trying to make a living. To the neophyte, they run the gamete...slim, fat, attractive, not so attractive, young, old, tall or short; everyday looking women.

It conjured up an experience that Miss Carolina and I had on a previous trip to Bangkok.

She likes to tell about our night at the old Calypso Club in Bangkok. It was touted as one of the best ladyboy shows in town, so of course, we were interested. The show lived up to its billing. Tall, gorgeous, young women with firm breasts and protruding buttocks in red sequined or white satin gowns. They all looked gorgeous and were obvious show stoppers. We were both as mesmerized as one could get even from the last row.

They were stunning. Las Vegas had nothing over these women and their professional production. Yes, women, because in my mind, I believed them to be so. There were no telltale signs of male masculinity. Each had long glistening, straight and natural jet-black hair, delicate features, soft shoulders, no Adams apples, pouty lips, and doe-like eyes. Yes, the eyes always got you. The hour-long show ended way too prematurely.

Miss Carolina encouraged me to have my picture taken with the performers after the show. She didn't have to ask me twice, but I only had one photograph taken. When we returned home, she showed me the dozens of pictures with me smiling like the town's simpleton. Funny, I don't recall those moments.

Katoys seems to be widely accepted as the third sex in Thailand. You can find them working as bank clerks, bakers, restaurant greeters, and government officials at border crossings and at every job imaginable including the world's oldest profession. My limited contact with Katoys has been positive.

Meanwhile, back at Starbucks, I found the staring and gawking by the three young tourists rather annoying and crossing the line.

They reminded me of zoo visitors taunting animals in their enclosures, making faces, and banging the cages. At this point, just who was really caged?

Pointing, staring, and laughing without regard for the feelings of others, I could take it no longer. I decided to take things into my own hands.

I stepped outside for a moment and motioned to the ladyboy to come and have coffee with me through a series of hand gestures.

She noticed, then looked to the left and her right and finally pointed a finger to herself as if to say, "me?" "Yes, yes," I nodded.

"I want to buy you a cup of coffee."

But selfishly, I really wanted to interview her for a story. Except to my surprise, "she" turned out not to be a "he." Na was a woman. She had a nine-year-old son. It was an honest mistake.

"Sorry, sorry, sorry…I am so sorry." I could not believe my gross mistake. Damn, why can't I tell the difference?

Things just don't always appear what they look like in Bangkok. But my mistaken identity with the ladyboy underscored an even greater life drama.

"Na," not her real name was funny, laughed a lot, and spoke very good English. She worked at the front desk of a small hotel, but the salary wasn't enough to help her family, especially during the rice harvest. So, she has taken to the streets of Bangkok to earn more money.

"I must make three hundred dollars in the next four days. I leave for home on the 20th. My father plants rice and I have to go home to help cut rice."

It is harvesting rice time in Thailand. All over the country, one sees tens of thousands of small rice paddies; a sea of green as far as one can see. Suddenly though, not all rice paddies seemed the same. In this case, the drama of impending doom was very real for Na and the extended family she supported.

Na will have to hire 20 people paying them 300 baht a day till all the rice was hand cut from the paddies. Her family of five will live on that rice crop in the coming year. Any left-overs will be their only source of income.

As the only daughter, Na sends money home to her parents and is the sole financial supporter for their wellbeing.

Research shows that the mythical average monthly salary of a working Thai is about $375.

The chance of Na making $300 in four days appears almost depressingly improbable.

Na thanked me for my kindness and soon returned to her spot in front of Starbucks. In the few hours that I observed her, she did not have a single customer. It will surely be a long and anxious next few days for her.

She was a grain of rice in a field of nameless workers in the Bangkok sex trade. I never saw her again.

That's Earle, brother

Bangkok, Thailand

La Ruta Maya

(La Ruta Maya or the Mayan Way takes readers through Guatemala and Honduras where some of the important Mayan civilizations were established such as Tikal and Copán. My stories came from the many people that I have befriended along the way and who may have been direct descendants of the Maya currently living in Central America.)

Don Federico

It is a homecoming of sorts; my fourth return visit to Isleta de Gaia, an oasis of an island hotel some seven thousand miles north of Antarctica where its pure air reaches Barra del Jiote unobstructed.

Don Federico brings out his mariner's compass to show us that Antarctica is exactly 180 degrees south of his island.

He has, over the last fifteen years, not only built his hotel but in the process made potable water, electricity, and sanitation available to the entire island. It was not a terribly difficult choice for him to have left his lifestyle in Paris, according to him that included rubbing shoulders with royalty and heads of states, as he had little or no time to really enjoy his life.

All his efforts in Guatemala were part of his dream to build a self-sustaining eco-lodge on a sliver of a sand bar that, at its widest, is only two hundred meters by seven kilometers long.

Barra del Jiote is now a haven for wealthy Guatemaltecos who flee the city on long weekends and head to this island accessible only by launch from nearby Las Lisas or helicopter from Guatemala City.

There are no shops, no roads, and no cars on the entire island. Hotel guests at his twelve, thatched-roof bungalows were often diplomats and North Americans looking for sanctuary at Isleta de Gaia.

Today, it is a mix of Guatemaltecos and foreigners on vacation, but home to dozens of permanent Guatemalan locals who are the maids, handymen, and housekeepers who provide the labor for those who can afford to maintain weekend homes here.

Long, solitary, and barefoot walks along its dark sandy beaches, the width of freeways, give the body an awareness that no hands-on massage can offer. The surf flattens out and washes your feet as sand recedes with the tide and you sink ever so slightly into your own footprint.

Each step takes you further into the fold of the island's allure.

A late afternoon, orange ball of fire cuts its way toward the horizon and you can become an audience of a few to behold sunsets that rival Maui's best. The brisk and unusually fresh southerly winds now shift to their evening speed and the sky brims brightly with more stars than both Hollywood and Bollywood combined.

One day while fishing, Don Federico was on to something. His fishing rod, bent to its breaking point, held something of great promise. What kind of fish was this? It must have been something huge. He recalled in English laced with a Parisian accent.

Then crowds of people started to line the beach watching this epic struggle unfold between man and beast, with no apparent end in sight.

As the crowds grew, so did the laughter. The people were on to something, which was not so evident to him. As they were sitting a few meters above sea level on a sand dune, pointing and laughing, it finally became clear. The giant fish at the end of his line turned out to be a giant 20 pound, brown Pacific pelican. Embarrassed at this spectacle, Don Federico hid out in his hotel till it was but a questionable dream.

As we smoked fresh Cohibas after a meal of "Lenguado ala Plancha" and rice laced by a ring of his small, home-grown, green limes, we shared stories long into the night while phosphorescent plankton glowed in the surf, not 50 meters away like so many stars reflecting off the water.

This corporate refugee left the business world of Paris and Singapore. He sold all his worldly possessions including his yacht, Paris apartments, expensive sports cars, and motorcycles, and built his dream on what was a waterless moonscape. The corporate world, however, had not forgotten Don Federico for occasionally, a private helicopter would land next to his property and friends would join him for "frijoles y arroz" and catching up.

Today, it is a very different place thanks to one man's vision and insistence. Don Federico has made his last stand here at Isleta de Gaia. It will be his home port for the last, long watch at the helm of his ship and in doing so will have brought about an improved way of living for many. It is inspiring to see what one person has done to make a difference in the lives of the island's permanent residents.

That's Earle, brother
Isleta de Gaia, Guatemala
2012

Post script:

My friend and humanitarian Don Federico did indeed command his last watch at the helm of Isleta de Gaia. While he passed away of breast cancer in Guatemala City, his spirit lives on at Barra del Jiote where the cool unobstructed air from Antarctica still blesses its shores.

My Husband Die Yesterday

Supichaya is a special needs teacher in Lampang Province in northern Thailand. She is one of my internet English students and a friend.

She had a class of about 35 students if you can imagine. Both of her children have recently finished their university studies and seemed well on their way to being financially independent.

She sent me an email this morning, "My husband die yesterday." I knew that her husband was not well and her ever so brief email was not really a surprise to me. Still, there was a sense of great sadness because her compassion and forgiveness are the real sources of her strength.

About 22 years ago, when her son and daughter were toddlers, her husband left them. Little was said. He walked out the door and had not been seen nor heard from since.

Several months ago, he knocked on her front door without warning. He had returned home. He was diagnosed with terminal cancer with only months to live. He asked her to care and comfort him during his waning days. He was alone.

"Nobody take care me."

Her response stunned me, but not before I presented this dilemma to family and friends. I was curious as to how we Westerners would respond given a similar set of circumstances. The responses from my informal survey were a unanimous, "NO."

"How can I refuse the father of my children," replied Supichaya.

Incredibly, she took him back and had cared for him since.

A few weeks ago, she shared this with me, "I not have any men in my life. Not have experience with men. One boyfriend then married. Never have problems with children, only husband young to old. Difficult raise two children alone. Can forgive him the less of his life." (sic)

I am continually amazed at the strength of women that I have met along the way from the pothole ridden streets of old Havana; to the cobblestoned, narrow alleys of the western highlands of Quezaltenango, Guatemala; from the towns like Udon Thani in Thailand and Luang Prabang, Laos; from the plains of old Bagan atop an ancient stupa in Burma and from the maze of side streets and alleys of the Old Quarter of Hanoi, Vietnam and even in my own backyard in Hawaii.

Women, all over the world, continue to impress me with their tales of strength, adversity, resolve, acts of compassion and kindness, and unwavering dedication to family.

My words to Supichaya were that she had taught her children a lesson of compassion and forgiveness in the scope that is rare even among great people.

The only unusual thing about my relationship with her is that we have never actually met in person. We have been friends for many years, but only through the internet.

I am, however, truly blessed to have had her share this personal story with me. I thought you might like to hear it also.

That's Earle, brother
Along the River of Dawn, Thailand
2013

Along the Ho Chi Minh Trail

During the Vietnam War, the Vietnamese supply line ran along Laos and Cambodia as well as in Vietnam. Stories from the Ho Chi Minh Trail represent those three countries.

Behind every face, there is a story. I do believe that. Whether it is a child selling trinkets in the streets of Antigua, Guatemala, or a disfigured beggar in the backstreets of Bangkok, if you stop and talk with them, they may share a story or two with you.

Sometimes you meet people by chance as I did one day when I took a flight from Los Angeles to Maui. I met a Vietnamese-American gal who was born in Vietnam but raised in the U.S. This is the story she told me. It is presented as best as I can remember.

The Cap

"Dad, what is it with that old baseball cap hanging under the lime tree in the back yard? It's all faded and torn...I'm throwing it away."

"Others have tried; they all failed. You will also. It's impossible. That old cap will always be with me. It was meant to be."

"It was then that my dad sat me down under that tree and retold his story again. I had heard it before but never tired of hearing it, much like a favorite fairy tale except in this case, it was true. I still remembered parts of it. I still recalled the fear of the cold, dark saltwater surrounding us on a moonless night and the strength of my dad holding our heads above water as we made our way out to the boat. I remembered as well as any seven-year-old can remember."

With no particular warning, with no particular urgency, my parents woke us up late one night in the village where all nine of us lived, my grandparents, mom and dad, and my three brothers and younger sister. I remember.

We were told to dress, two shirts, one over the other. The same for our underwear and pants. One pair of shoes was all that I took and like everyone else, we stole into the night, walking in single file along the rice paddies without a sound, without a single bag among us.

It was that quiet hour when all you heard was the silent stillness and the croaking of frogs. It was the sound of the village sleeping, the sound of spirits at rest. There were no goodbyes to friends or relatives. It was an abrupt departure; we knew not where we were heading.

We walked for hours, but no one complained. My grandparents were old, but they tried to keep pace. We stayed together and we vowed that we would always be together when we finally reached our embarkation point.

A small wooden boat, barely able to hold more than forty people was already over capacity and jammed with its silent human cargo. Steadily, we pushed our way on board; suddenly, there is a commotion behind us, and voices of panic and anxiety rang out.

People shouted, "Quickly, into the boat! Everyone, push off!" But not all of us made it. Grandpa and grandma were left behind. To me, they died on the beach for we never saw them again. They were arrested and sentenced to spend the rest of their lives in a North Vietnamese prison.

We escaped, but it was 1979 and as Vietnamese citizens of Chinese ancestry, we were still unwelcome in Vietnam. We were outsiders even though we were born in South Vietnam, spoke fluent Vietnamese and even changed the spelling of our name to be more acceptable to hardline Communists.

My dad was a wise man with a strong sense of family. I always remembered him saying that we would stay together; we would live together and when we leave, we would leave together.

On that small boat to freedom, everybody pressed against each other. There was no room to move, least stand or take a few steps. We just lay there in the scorching sun and chilly nights like so much cargo. When we had to go, we did our business right there where we lay. But if it was number two, then dad would use his cap and somehow toss the contents overboard. This portable potty was all that the seven of us had.

When we finally reached our destination, we were clueless about our location nor did we care much at that point. We just wanted off that boat.

Our wobbly legs were uncontrollable and we fell on the sand as we ran from the boat. "Here, Mr. Chuong (not his real name), you forgot your hat." Someone handed my dad his now wretched cap. We landed on a secluded beach somewhere in Malaysia. It was supposed to be a refugee camp, but there was no camp, no tents, no food, no shelter, and no water. It was just a beach surrounded by dense jungle. We were to be refugees for a year.

My dad was a resourceful person for he quickly climbed a coconut tree and got us food and drink. It was to be our main source of sustenance for much of the year. He built us a shack using woven palm fronds and sticks from the jungle. We lived like Tom Hanks in the Castaway.

Every other month or so, a plane would land bringing supplies wherein ensued a mad scramble to get on the plane when it was void of cargo and returning to Australia or America, or who knew where. With luck, you just jumped on a plane and trusted your future to a roll of the dice.

We could have taken the first few planes, but it would have meant separating the family. My dad wouldn't have it and so we dejectedly walked away several times. The elation of seeing a plane land was countered by the deep emptiness at seeing it leave without us. When a plane finally came with room for our entire family, it was a race to get on board, but dad got each of us in the plane first, then mom and he last. We left with just the rags that we wore.

Just as they were closing the door, a man pulled the door open. "Mr. Chuong, you forgot your cap." It had returned to him a second time in just as dramatic a moment. That stinky, dirty, faded cap would not leave his side.

I am forty-one now, a professional freelance photographer and my entire family still live in Hawaii. Like the survivors that they were, my parents worked at multiple jobs, saved, bought a house, and got each and every one of us educated and today, we are as successful as anyone in the country.

We are living the American Dream, but with the memory that the journey was not without a price. I place flowers beside the family altar every morning to let my grandparents know that they are not forgotten.

So when I tried to throw dad's cap away for the umpteenth time, I knew what he was going to say. But then, I would never have thrown it away either. It would come back to us. It is a reminder that as successful a life that we live today, none of it came easily.

That's Earle, brother
On a flight to Maui
2014
https://www.ricetreechronicles.com

A Road North and South

I met Antonio in Guatemala. Young, personable, but on the quiet side, he shared his journey after we got to know each other over several days. Like others before him, he found the way North but also found his way back home.

"Doors work both ways," according to Gunji's Manual and as I have learned, so do roads. This was rediscovered after speaking with Antonio from Guatemala. Here is his story as I remembered it through our conversation in Spanish.

In many ways, his journey North was similar to several other Guatemaltecos that I have met over the years. Four other men and women come to mind and together their stories became one. Names and locations have been altered in my stories.

"You know," Antonio told me, "I was 27 years old and had always dreamed about going North. I was married and had three children. There was no future for me here, so I decided to go North after saving and borrowing money from friends and family."

"I left Quetzaltenango in the western highlands and walked across the border into Mexico. Several weeks later, I came to the border between the U.S and Mexico, but the crossing was not going to be an easy one. I had to cross the Sonoran Desert first.

"Nor was it cheap. The Mexican coyotes wanted $4,000 upfront to guide me through the desert. We slept at night and walked during the day. One old man in our group could not keep up and I think he died in the desert, but I kept thinking of my wife and the oldest boy who cried on the phone the night before I left…'don't go papa…please don't go.' I cried too."

"He didn't understand. Here, I had nothing, but there in America, with hard work, I could earn money and maybe get some land and build a house. It was my dream."

"It took me almost a week of walking. It was hot. We had very little water and even less food and shade. The nights were awfully cold, but it was for my family that I went. Twice helicopters passed overhead so we dove under the mesquite trees for cover. Luckily, we were not discovered.

"The actual crossing of the U.S. Border happened at night. It was the easiest part. Getting caught soon after, however, was not the ending that I had in mind. It made me sad and I was immediately arrested, finger-printed, photographed, and deported. They sent me back by bus across the Mexican border. What took days took just hours for the return trip.

"Three days later, I attempted the desert crossing again. Yes, it was crazy, but I was young and determined. This time, the results were different. The coyotes stayed with us and arranged for us to go to Pittsburgh by car. They wanted another $3,000. Even though it cost me $7,000 and 35 days of trekking, my dream had been realized. I was in Pennsylvania."

"Till this day, I don't know where it is on the map, but I lived there for two years working three jobs. One was full-time with McDonald's, a part-time job with a stone factory, and another in a hotel/restaurant. I washed dishes."

"In total, I worked 16 hours a day, every day, no holidays, no sick days, but I was happy. Sometimes, I only slept four hours, but I saved. Some others that I knew, got accustomed to the easy life and started to spend more than they made, but I kept thinking of my children and my wife back in Guatemala."

"You know what Papi, the roads lead North, but they also lead South. It goes both ways and thanks to God, I found my way back."

"Funny thing though, it only cost me $450 to fly back to Guatemala."

I was puzzled. "Didn't they hassle you because you were an illegal?

"What about a passport?"

"No Papi, going South is easy; going North, not so much."

I continued. "And how are you doing today?"

"Today, I have a small piece of land thanks to Sr. Federico of Isleta de Gaia, and I have built a house. I have a job here at his hotel which not many can say.

"My oldest son, the one who cried and begged me not to leave, is now in a private school in the next municipality. He is very smart."

"I am happy the way things turned out. I am one of the lucky ones for sure."

"Yes, Antonio. Leaving is good, but coming home is even better isn't it."

That's Earle, brother
Somewhere in Guatemala
2015

The Benevolent Man

Driving a cab all day doesn't sound like a job one would likely look forward to each and every day but like any other line of work, it is what we make of it. For many, I suspect, that's all that it is, a job, but for those whose personalities and inclinations lean toward people rather than things, it can be a whole new world.

On a long drive into the countryside, my driver, who spoke quite a bit of English mixed in with Thai, regaled me with the tales from his 30+ years behind the wheel in Bangkok.

"I love job. Wake up every day, it is different you know. Not same same. One day can write book some people I meet. When you drive, must remember where to go, what to get, who go where. I not forget maybe come back again. If people like, maybe tell friend. I make friend again."

He was a rolly polly kind of guy with an accompanying laugh that came deep from within. You could tell his sincerity, and I was genuinely interested in what he had to say and how he said it. I wasn't sure which was more amusing, but he certainly had tales to share. This was an instance where the destination didn't really matter, but the journey was interesting.

The Kind Falang

"One guy from America, he was 50+. He wants to go to Lanna area to find a girlfriend. I say OK...I know. A driver must know everywhere, everything because customers want. So I tell him, OK, we go. I take him anywhere in Thailand. He meets nice lady. They talk long time. He gone home with lady. Stay with girl family. I go back Bangkok. I think everyone happy."

"One week later, he calls. My friend, I need your help. I think he have trouble. OK, mai pen rai (no problem). Long drive that time, but that time I have power. When meet, he says he want to buy refrigerator for family...can can. Buy refrigerator. Then he wants stove for cook for girl's mother. Can can...we go. After go girl house talk with family. I speak Thai. He speaks English...everything OK."

"He tell girl, he not want her working in bar. She promises not to work anymore. He goes back to Bangkok. Every month he sends girl money. Two year he does. Never forget. Later his company send him another country. Ooh, trouble. (Laughs) He not send money to girlfriend One year. Then come back Bangkok. He calls me. OK we go look for your girlfriend."

"One more time, long drive to Lanna country. Find girl. Now she dark, dark skin. How come? Why she so dark? Hand skin very bad. I ask girl. She tells me, he not send money. Have to work help family. But she makes promise to him not go back bar work. She goes work one to one and a half year in building labor. She carry bricks every day. Work 10 hours every day. Never go back bar."

"I tell him story. He crying, crying. She crying, crying. I crying too. But they happy. He happy. Ok, he say to girlfriend, You get ready, you not go back construction tomorrow, not go back bar. Stay together with me."

"I think they marry. This Falang have good heart. In Thai we say, jai dee mak (very good heart)."

Remember me?

"One time Japan man come Bangkok. He, I think architect about 50. Maybe young, maybe old, cannot tell Japanese man. I think he have money. Give big money that time many years ago. He ask me special request. Only want young girl not know another man. Driver must know everything for customer. So I thinking. I say to him, can check. Call back tomorrow. OK, he call again next day."

"OK, I find for you. Can choose from one or two. But we go long drive in country. Oh, I tell you have two young girls. One very pretty, other one not so much. He looking, looking. He want one girl first night. Pretty girl, he want second night. OK, I go back Bangkok. I say call me if need help."

"One week later, he call me. My friend, come back. He like this pretty young girl. Go take her back Japan marry. She not know anything. She is young and from the country. I tell her, if man give you money you must save. Never spend money. Put away. Save money. Don't forget what I tell you. One year, two year maybe everything OK. But never know. Sure, sure? She say yes. Thank you papa she tell me."

"Twenty year later, I am airport taxi driver at Suvarnabhumi Airport Bangkok. This beautiful lady come my cab. She want ride to country. OK, mai pen rai. We going, going. Only small talk. She ask me, you not remember me? I was the number 2 girl long time ago."

"I look this pretty lady. Sia jai, sorry, sorry. I don't remember."

"When I was young, I went to Japan with my husband and I grew up. We buy small business shop, now have many business in Japan. I go visit my family. Help family build house for cousin and father and mother. Twenty years ago. You helped me. You gave me good advice like a father. I nevah forget you."

"Ooh, I tell you that day good day for me."

My driver had many stories over that full day of driving. One could see that it was more than a job. He was genuinely interested in bringing people together, giving advice when needed, being there and going out his way to accommodate his passengers. He was a social worker, financial advisor, friend and match maker all in one.

Yes, every day was different for him and he has been driving for fifty years. I wish I had booked him for a week of stories.

That's Earle, brother
Bangkok, Thailand
www.ricetreechronicles.com

Erik the Red
(The Rest of the Story)

I don't often resend a story out to friends, but I am making an exception in this instance. Sometimes, there is "the rest of the story" that caps off an initial one. I believe that this is the case here. The full original story starts here, followed by the epilogue and "three years later." It'll bring you up to date on one man's story.

On a small soi in northeastern Thailand, I spotted an unusually tall falang (Caucasian foreigner) eating ice cream.

"Hi! That ice cream any good?"

"It's the best, man."

"I come here every day and this guy," pointing to the vendor, "knows me well, speaks a little English, and makes the best coconut ice cream in Khon Kaen."

"Well, those two kids next to you seem to enjoy it; they look pretty happy."

A cute brother and sister of about 8–10 years old contentedly seemed to be in ice cream heaven and quickly darted back into the safety of their mother's laundry shop which was only feet away from the ice cream vendor.

"Yeah, I come by here twice a day. Every afternoon, the ice cream guy waits for me. He knows my schedule."

"See the gal in there? That's her laundry business. Her name is Noon. You know, morning, noon, and night," then chuckles to himself.

"She works every day till three in the morning; she washes clothes, irons and folds. She is one hard-working lady, and so is her mom.

"Her two kids are really nice. I like them a lot.

"They all live here (now pointing to a small shop); all sleep in this cramped one-room shop; two on the floor and two sharing that small cot over there. They eat sitting on the floor then they go to school and come back and do their homework here.

"The kids are really well behaved and polite."

For a big guy, the stranger seemed very soft-spoken and gentle in his ways. I learned that his name was Erik.

"Yes, they seem to be, Erik. I've brought my laundry here before and they are a nice, friendly family. I even took my laundry home yesterday and forgot to pay them but quickly returned with the money. The mom, who spoke no English at all, told me, "mai pen rai" not to worry. She was all smiles."

"How long you've been in Thailand, Erik?"

"Going on three years Papi and for the last year, I've been coming to this shop every day."

"Once a week, I buy the kids a bag of goodies. It's so cheap; it's not a problem, and they love it."

"I tell Noon, if you ever want a boyfriend, you tell me when you ready. I will build you a house. Your mother and children will have a home, and you can drive to work instead of sleeping here."

"You know Papi, I've been an orphan since I was three. I never had a real family before. I'm kinda ready for a family now. It would be nice."

"Well, any luck Erik?"

"Not yet, but I keep trying…(a smile lit up his face)."

"By the way, where are you from?"

"Inner-city Detroit. I used to be in federal law enforcement."

My ears perked up as he would have been the kind of guy my buddy Ranger Mike would like meeting. Mike was also a federal law enforcement officer as well, though working with much better constituents in the U.S. National Park Service.

"Oh, what branch?"

"DEA. Yeah, it was getting a little hairy and after getting shot four times and stabbed twice, I figured that I was pushing my luck, so I retired."

"Well, yeah Erik, look at your clientele and you probably were about six inches taller than most of your teammates…big target, you know."

We both laughed.

"Yeah, guess I was an easy target. Just before retiring, I had to chase a guy down and when I got him, I was totally wiped out. I was 320 pounds at the time. I'm 6'5", so I didn't show it. I didn't have a belly you know, but I knew something had to change if I was going to retire.

"This nutritionist that I consulted, promised me that I would lose 150 pounds in two years if I followed his regiment to the letter. No sugar, no alcohol, no meat, low carbs, no white rice; totally vegetarian."

"Erik, I couldn't do that, I was raised in Hawaii. We eat rice every day.

"My wife still doesn't understand why I need rice at every meal."

"Well, replied Erik, I walk about 8–10 miles every day. I'm religious about what goes into my body, and I've lost 150 pounds with one month to spare."

"Well, you look great Erik."

He pulled his shirt tightly from behind.

"I'm down to a 32-inch waist."

He really did look great, in his green, Tommy Bahamas pineapple Aloha shirt, and Bermuda-type shorts. He was a handsome dude with fading red hair that lit up like a flame against the setting sun.

"You know what Erik, since coming here, I've been riding my motorbike too much. You are inspiring me to walk more which is what I really like to do. It's just that a motorbike is so much fun, and I can get to places quicker, especially when it's hot."

He added, "Walking is great and you see so much."

"Well, I wish you luck. I hope things go your way, Erik."

Erik seemed a likable, regular kind of guy. He went to the laundry shop twice a day. He ate the same vegetarian breakfast every day at the same time in the same place. He says, even the two gals running the food stall liked his stuff so much, they are now selling it as per his recipe.

He returned to the laundry every afternoon with railroad precision to buy coconut ice cream for himself (his only vice) and Noon's kids then asked her if she was ready for a boyfriend. His ritual ends on that same note every afternoon.

With that kind of routine discipline, I am sure Erik will eventually have the family he has always wanted. I sure hope so.

That's Earle, brother
Khon Kaen, Thailand
2015

Epilogue 2015

After several days of getting to know Erik (not his real name), I think I may have a bead on his stalled love life. He must either have a dozen of the same double extra-large Tommy Bahama shirts that now hang baggily on his tall, lanky frame, or he is in dire need to have Noon do his laundry.

Three years later, 2018: I first wrote this story and shared it with friends in 2015, but I went back to revisit the place. I wanted to find out if there was a..." the rest of the story." It is February 2018, and I stopped by to see my friend who owned a spa next door to Noon's laundry shop. The laundry shop was no longer there and seemed to be under some kind of major renovation. I asked my friend about it. She told me that Noon got married to some tall Falang.

"I know who," I replied with a smile and felt in my heart that Erik the Red was successful after all.

Erik was the kind of guy that you just wanted to root for. I found myself being a fan of his and hoping that he'd hit a home run of sorts. As it turns out, I guess old fashion fairy tales can still happen and coconut ice cream and persistence can make dreams come true.

That's Earle, Brother
Khon Kaen, Thailand
2018

Maui No Ka Oi

Maui No Ka Oi translates to "Maui is the best" and offers stories from the late 40's to the present covering several islands.

When All My Heroes
Were Cowboys

Saturdays were the best day of the week for me. I grew up on Market Street in Wailuku remembering Saturday mornings with great anticipation of adventure, of doing good and of putting away the bad guys with Western justice. In the 1950s when Hawaii was still a territory, I knew who was despicable and who was to be revered. The movies taught me that. It was part and parcel for every boy growing up at the time. Life was understandable then.

The center of the universe, as I saw it, revolved around the Iao Theater in the center of Market Street, which was not only the Mecca of all that was holy and good but also the source of justice and the cowboy way.

It was, after all, where all my heroes lived on the big screen in screaming black and white but stored in my mind as vivid living color. I was highly influenced by the King of Cowboys, Roy Rogers who himself was greater than life. He once came to Puunene on his way to Hana, Maui, and brought along his horse Trigger. There was no mention of Dale Evans, but then again, who cared. I was eight years old.

My dad drove us down to the old Hawaiian Airlines terminal soon after it was converted from the Naval Air Station/U.S. Army Air Corps strip into the commercial airports of Hawaiian and Trans-Pacific Airlines. There, my hero was driven back and forth before a hysterical posse of cap pistol-toting, hat-waving mini cowboys. It was the best day of my life.

But it was the Saturdays that had the greatest impact on my life. Iao Theater always had a kiddie show at 9:00 in the morning...rain or shine. It was my sacred duty not to miss the show. After all, it featured three cartoons, an occasional travelogue which I and my friends booed soundly while tossing boiled peanut shells at the screen.

The absolute worst thing to show before the main feature would have been a sing-along flick with a bouncing white ball to the tune of Moonlight Bay. It was worse than having to drag your kid sister to the movies with you.

Seasonally, a Yoyo contest would be held with World Champion Barney Akers on stage performing his double-handed loop the loop trick as we counted out aloud while we sat at the edges of our seats grasping our Duncan Yoyos. Of course, everything prior to the main feature was mere appetizers. They were all part of the kaleidoscope of treats leading up to a western. All two hours of this holy endeavor for only nine cents.

It was during those early Saturday mornings at the Iao Theater that I was introduced to Whip Wilson, Gene Autry, Lash RaLue, Hop Along Cassidy, one of my all-time favorites, and of course Roy.

To anyone else, they were just Hollywood actors. But to me, they were anything but, they were my moral compass. They taught me to be polite as in taking off my hat in front of a lady, opening the doors for the women, and saying, "yes, ma'am or thank you ma'am."

Of course, a lasting lesson that I learned was that you only used your pistol to shoot the gun out of the bad guy's hand. You never shot a guy in the back. It was the rule of the West and every wannabe buckaroo this side of market street knew that. Roy would have been proud had he known that.

Even in fighting, I learned a lot through the movies. You had to chase down the bad guy first and only then lasso him off his horse which of course was never white like Topper or a Palomino like Trigger. It was only then that you engaged the bad guy in a "mano a mano" brawl, subdued him, and brought him to justice. I loved every bit of the "pow" and "thump" that my heroes meted out. There could be only one conclusion, the good guy always won fair and square. The best part though was that his white hat, somehow, never fell off his head.

Yes, Saturdays at the Iao Theater were the best days of the week. It was a good time in my life when all my heroes were cowboys and on the way home, you could get a manapua from Hashimoto's Okazuya.

That's Earle, brother
Wailuku, Maui, Hawaii T.H.
www.ricetreechronicles.com

The Great Escape

Kindergarten at Wailuku Elementary School was the beginning of my formal education. Although much wasn't said at home, I always knew that school was important. I guess it was an unwritten rule in our family as it was for many families at the time.

You'd wash up on a Monday morning, put on a freshly starched Aloha shirt so stiff that you had to gingerly break your arms through the sleeves. If you had gone to the beach the day before, then it would have been sheer torture and your shirt felt like sandpaper over your sunburnt back. It was a mild form of self-mutilation most commonly reminiscent of Monday mornings.

Before leaving our small two-bedroom, flat-roofed house on Wells Street, a quick inspection by my mother meant that all was right and ready to go.

My sister and I walked the three blocks up Wells Street barefoot and happy to be on our way to school. No one really wore shoes or slippers. In fact, I never wore shoes to school until the eighth grade and only because I became socially aware of what others were wearing. Peer pressure sometimes worked wonders.

Wailuku Elementary School still stands today where I have always remembered it. The prominent granite administration building was built from stones gathered from Iao Valley and neighboring plantation fields. Mrs. Bucek was the principal and rumor had it that you would never want to be called into her office. There in the lower left hand drawer of her large roll top oak desk was where she kept her twelve-foot bullwhip. Woe be the kid who got called into her office for some kind of mischief.

But the year was 1948 and I was in kindergarten where the biggest task for the day was to build something with the giant two by four blocks of wood. No silly Legos, we had the real stuff with blocks ranging anywhere from several inches to a foot and a half in length.

We built structures like post offices and giant boats that resembled Noah's Ark and when completed, the reward was being allowed to sleep in them during nap time. There was finger painting with some warm gooey stuff that felt good oozing between your fingers and playing instruments like tambourines and triangles during music time.

All these activities took a bit out of us kids and so nap time was a welcomed relief. As we crawled into our home-sewn denim sleeping bags along with matching eye bands visions of recess and snacks danced through our heads.

One day, for reasons I do not remember, several of us were allowed to take our nap in the small back room facing the cane field. It was a rare privilege. In the privacy of the back room, some kid named Kama-thought it would be great if we all sneaked out through the back window, ran up the embankment, and hide in the cane field. A great idea!

Slowly and quietly like cane mice, we climbed out the window and hid. After nap time, out came Miss. Nansy with the rest of the class in tow. There would be a showdown. Someone had to give in, but it was not going to be me.

One by one, my gang of five dwindled to four then three and finally one. Our fearless leader Kama gave us up. He was the first one down...that rat! But I resisted. I held out and remained alone. "OK, Mr. Earle, I guess you will just have to miss cookies and milk for snack today," at which she and the class did an immediate about-face and headed back to the classroom.

"Wait, cookies and milk? Snack time? I forgot the most important thing of the day...after nap snacks...wait...WAIT...I'm coming! I'm sorry Miss. Nansy, I'm sorry. I'm sorry."

Those were my hard lessons in life and for a five-year-old, what better motivation than cookies and milk. My great escape soon faded into oblivion as my bare feet carried me obediently back to the classroom after my teacher.

That's Earle, brother
Wailuku, Maui, Hawaii
Circa 1948

The Road to Havana

All stories are from Havana, Cuba over a period of two years.

If She Could Only Cook

"Un cafesito con leche por favor." The dark roast Serra went down easily and I eased back in my chair to take in the now-familiar sounds of the early morning. The streets are still empty at seven; the Old City is still asleep behind locked doors. The doors themselves are barricades of ornate wrought iron works of art and unlike their intent to keep the unwanted out, really would quietly draw people to its durable beauty.

It is surprisingly quiet on Calle Compostela with only the sound of palm frond brooms being swept across its cobblestone streets. An occasional church bell peals accompanied by a chorus of roosters and dogs. The city is awakening.

From a third-floor apartment booms a voice to a lone figure on the street below.

"Dona Ailise...do you have cooking oil to spare?"

"No Maribelle, but I have some sugar."

"OK, I'll pass the bucket down."

This simple bucket and rope trick works well and neighbors share what little they may have and somehow, they make do.

My young friend Marcus Antonio pulled out a Bic pen. "This is for you my friend," he said as he handed it to a local constable. This pen wasn't a souvenir, but a valued item as are cigarette lighters, powdered milk, a bar of soap..." everything is so expensive here and so hard to come by." Eraldo (I am known as 'Eraldo' in Spanish and Portuguese speaking countries), see this pharmacy here? There is little on the shelves, but look across the street to the Pharmacy for 'estrangeros,' it is full. You know, it is a wonderful thing that we have free health care. We never have to pay for anything, except medicines, but then, who can afford that."

Tucked away in the corner behind a low-standing wall, Carlito Sanchez caressed his trumpet-like his favorite lady. He learned to play it by listening to his neighbor. He never studied music, but his soulful sounds echoing through the streets near the Plaza de Armas draw a small and appreciative crowd. "You know, Winston Marsalis stopped by and gave me a gift. I play from my heart..." I nod in agreement. I enjoy his company and his banter with visitors and part company after an hour.

One evening while walking near the Plaza de San Francisco de Asis, I struck up a conversation with a young, attractive, dark-eyed university student majoring in Agriculture. She was already in her third year. "You know, my mother is also a teacher like you, but she is suffering from Liver cancer. I cannot afford to buy her medicine.

"Señor, I will sleep with you for sixty dollars."

"I am sorry chica, thank you, but no."

"I will do anything…"

Her voice now trembling and her eyes tearing; it was gut-wrenching. She appeared only a few years older than my students and clearly seemed to be wrestling with her decision. I turn away so she could not see the tears in my eyes.

"You do not have to do this. There are other options." But I have none to offer. Clearly, I do not comprehend the hardships and realities that they face.

"Here, here is something…it may help. It is not much." I hand her five dollars, and we part company. I never saw her again, but I wish that I had given her more. It is, as friend Dave has said more than once, it is the things that we didn't do that give us the most regrets in life.

I have reminded myself that in life, I will come by each day, each moment only once, and any chance to do some good must be done then for I will never have that moment again.

The hand-cut stone pavements and the narrow-one lane streets are lined with an assortment of Chevys from the late forties and early fifties, iconic Buicks with their chrome teeth, and an occasional, vintage Mercedes 190.

"You know Papi," Karel told me one evening with his head, still under the hood of his 1956(?) Mercedes, "I spend most of my time with her. I take care of her. I pamper her and talk to her in a soft, sweet voice…'mi amor.' What little money that I can make, goes to make her run better."

"Yes, if she only could cook…aaaah. Ha ha ha ha…I wouldn't need anything else!"

There are challenges here no doubt, but people find a way. They dig down deep, share what little they have, and look out for each other. Some will make good choices and for some the choices will be made for them. Some choose to live by a stricter standard, while others may choose to live on the edge of deep shadows. It is quiet again. The dimly lit streets are not threatening at all even late at night when the barrio sleeps.

I feel safer here than almost anywhere else in the Americas. A few residents still whisper in the doorways and shadows of Calle Compostela and once again, I find myself at Doña Estela's house. I am home.

That's Earle, brother
Old Habana, Cuba
2013

A Man-Eating Crocodile

There are crocodiles in Vietnam as well as in neighboring Cambodia and Laos. There are two here, the Siamese and the Saltwater Crocodiles. Here's how they line up.

It is said that "Salties" run-up to twenty feet and can weigh in at a ton. The small Siamese crocs commonly grow up to 13 feet, large enough to inflict serious damage to two-legged visitors like me.

The last known wild Siamese croc was found recently, dead, apparently garroted by poachers. It was estimated that she was over 100 years old. I guess some men are not afraid of "Crocodylus Siamensis" but I know that I am.

For that reason alone, I have forsaken all rivers and lakes in the world, even the Nuuanu Réservoir in Hawaii. I refuse to be a victim to a man-eating crocodile.

Either by rumor or in fact, there apparently have been one or two cases of man-eating tigers in Vietnam and possibly one case where a man-eating croc tried to devour a Viet Cong soldier. I don't know the truth about all of this, but it got my attention. All the more reason to stay a landlubber for sure.

Oh, the threat is real my friends. Two years ago, at Dinh Binh town, Vietnam, the Kim Dong School was closed when wandering crocs threaten some students. Apparently, they had developed a taste for elementary school children or teachers.

As I am a former teacher, I could surely be on their menu. Hence, my apprehension about crocodiles. It's not that I lose any sleep over these man-eaters, but one can't be overly cautious even on dry land. Haven't you heard of the crocodiles that live in the sewers of NYC?

So, one can either be a victim or choose not to be. I have chosen the later and taken a positive step toward eliminating any threat of being eaten alive by a man-eating crocodile.

In fact, just last night at dinner in the Old Quarter of Hanoi, my friend Bill chose the Rack of Lamb while I opted for the exotic, farm-raised crocodile. Simply put, it was a case of a man-eating crocodile. That'll show 'em.

That's Earle, brother
Fine dining in Hanoi, Vietnam
2014
www.ricetreechronicles.com

I Heard It on the Camino

In a little village on the Camino, I stopped by the only mercadito (small market) on the road in this out-of-the-way pueblo of about 30 people and, as it was not busy, struck up a conversation with Sra. Maria Carmen. She was a pleasant woman with a warm smile and she asked where I was from.

"From Hawaii."

"Señor, you are the first person I see from Hawaii. Hawaii beautiful, yes? Sometimes my husband speaks of Hawaii, but that was a long time ago."

"I tell you something interesting, Señor."

"Si, Señora!"

She continued. "Many years ago, I was visiting my sick mother in the hospital in a nearby town. I went every day to see her."

"One day, the police found an old man. He was lost. He didn't have papers. Nothing. He didn't even know where he was nor who he was."

"A policeman told me the hospital couldn't take him. He wasn't sick."

"The police asked me, 'Sra Carmen, you have a big house, and your husband died long time already. Can you take him in?'"

"Impossible," I replied. But I felt pity for him.

"What will the neighbors say? I have a store to run."

"Well Señor, that was years ago. He is still here."

"Papa," calling the old gentleman working the shelves; check the back room for deliveries."

"I want the bread out, Gracias."

The old man in the rear of the market was so quiet that I had not noticed him silently shuffling along.

She continued, "He is my savior. He doesn't say much. Sometimes, he even speaks in another language. He is a quiet man. He has a good heart. He is all I have now."

"A few years ago, a woman from America was on the Camino with her daughter. I think this lady was nearly 80."

"The daughter was asking about a lost person. From an old, yellowish envelope, she showed me a black and white picture of a young couple on their honeymoon in Hawaii. They looked happy together."

"Señor, I was shocked. I thought the man in the picture was my husband.

"Wait here." I told them and went to the back of the store and brought my husband."

"He looked at them with a blank stare. Nothing. Silence. Then he went back to the shelves without saying a word."

"I could see tears in their eyes. I don't know if my husband knew them. You know his memory had vanished a long time ago."

"Oh, it hurt me so much. I thought they might take him away."

"The daughter replied, "No, Señora, we are mistaken."

"The old woman remained silent."

"We think my father died somewhere on the Camino. But no one ever found him.

"Your husband is not my father. My dad would have recognized us."

"My mother never remarried after my father disappeared. His last words to her were in a hand-written letter. He said that if he were to die on the Camino he wanted to be buried there."

"We are looking for his grave or a sign that maybe he came by this way."

"I was crying and I said, "If your father was on the Camino, he was in a happy place."

"The daughter continued, "We have been blessed on this Pilgrimage by all the wonderful people we have met.""

It is not uncommon to see posters like this along the Camino de Santiago of missing persons.

"God bless you Señora Carmen, and God Bless your husband too."

"They hugged me then they both hugged my husband for a very long time…"

I heard it on the Camino.

That's Earle, brother

On the Camino de Santiago, Spain

2016

I Smile Like I Was Twenty
All Over

The mornings in the Old City come quickly and the heat as well. Seeking shade from the buildings in the narrow alleyways offered tranquility and refuge from the blistering Cuban sun.

Passing by the old, neglected neighborhoods with their sad but wrinkled colonial facades with chickens running in and out of homes and garbage still in the street, there still was what appeared to be signs of change in the air. In the "calles," it became more evident.

Here in a triangulated crossroad, not more than the size of a twenty-five-meter pool fronting the Iglesia del Santo Angel, Jacqueline, a doctor by training and now entrepreneur along with her colleagues have revitalized one small footprint in the Old City.

By taking abandoned buildings, anchoring a Boutique/Coffee shop in one corner, lining the square in cobbled stone, giving a fresh coat of paint to the buildings, setting up umbrella tables for restaurant clients and visitors have together helped to create a sense of hope.

People come, residents and visitors, not to just see the adjacent church nor because Jacqueline has infused this small part of the city with a facelift, but because others have bought into the dream. Now there are family-sized boutique hotels and bicycle taxi stands nearby. It is becoming a neighborhood magnet.

"It was horrible and unsafe, especially at night. You could not imagine how bad it was. I should know," said long-time resident Rafael. "I was born right there," pointing to the small blue corner house.

Early morning brought the neighbors out into the streets where concrete benches and potted plants lined its borders. Neighbors like Doñas Madeleine, Selma, Mina, and Nita chat on the steps and housewives heading to the market somehow find a reason to make a detour through this tiny oasis.

As the morning progressed, so did occasional groups of visitors, some English speaking, some Spanish. This personal entrepreneurial dream had a soft side as it should have; making a positive change in people's lives through changes in the environment. It was Costner's Field of Dreams. If you build it, they will come.

As you sit in the square, watching mothers push their strollers, vendors passing by, bicycle taxi riders pushing their vehicles up the small incline, and school children in their red shorts and skirts with white tops and matching red scarves all moving with a quickened pace. The heartbeat here is palpable.

"Si Papi, I was born just there." Doña Clara pointed a bent, coffee-colored finger down the street.

I met Clara in a Casa de Abuelos (senior living home) sitting in a rocker behind a wrought iron window facing the street. It was a room full of forgotten memories and blank stares. She was the only one with a sparkle in her eyes.

With the sun still high in the sky, I decided to stop. A smile and "Buenas Dîas," brought her to her feet, and she quickly made her way to the door to greet me.

I introduced myself and we chatted a bit.

"I love it here; Habana Vieja (Old Havana). It was more beautiful when I was a little girl. I am 89 years old, and when the city sleeps, I think of it, and I smile like I was twenty all over."

That just about describes how I feel also, Doña Clara. You made me feel 20 all over.

That's Earle, brother
Habana Vieja, Cuba
2015

The Road to Bali

The "Road to Bali" was the title of an old Bing Crosby and Bob Hope film along with Dorothy L'amour although filmed entirely in a Hollywood film lot. There are some 18,000 islands in the Indonesian Archipelago and stories were gathered from Java, Bali, Borneo, Sulawesi, Flores and Komodo Islands

The "Opihi" Man of Makassar

Sulawesi (Formerly known as the Celebes in the Greater Sunda Islands, Indonesia.)

Beycha: A three-wheeled pedicab where the passengers sit in front. Used for short hauls in many cities, but banned in Jakarta.

Little did I know, but this morning I was destined to go into a business venture with someone whom I had not yet met.

My beycha driver, soon to be friend and guide for all practical purposes, had attached himself to me like an "opihi" (sea limpet). In Hawai'i, these single-shelled mollusks cling tenaciously to boulders on rocky shores. Any amount of prying them off takes serious effort.

He had conveniently planted himself at Fort Rotterdam, the most recognizable landmark in Makassar. Its history goes back to the sixteen century and continued when the Dutch built it and maintained their stranglehold on Sulawesi.

The Opihi Man was sitting inside with no tourists anywhere in sight. In fact, it was so strange that I seemed to be the only visitor in town, not that I was, but I had yet to come across any foreign visitors, Asian or otherwise elsewhere on the island.

But while touring the fort, I encountered no one who was able to speak any English. There was a guide sitting in the snack shop, but he was too busy getting checkmated by everyone he played against. It was only an amiable beycha driver who apparently was available.

So the Opihi Man, in his easy-going manner, tried to get me to ride his beycha and go to the fish market, small boat harbor, big boat harbor; any place that had an abundance of fish and boats.

Sporting a grin from ear to ear, he said, "Have fis, plenty fis; if no fis, no pay."

I was more interested in walking to the fish market than riding there.

"I want to walk to the fish market."

"Too far mister, over seven kilometers."

"But I like to walk."

Sometimes, I walk twenty kilometers a day, although the Opihi Man wouldn't have known that, but something told me that today was not to be one of those days. For over a mile and a half, he shadowed me on his rig; me walking on the street or segments of what appeared to be sidewalks and he, on the pavement alongside me.

"OK, mister, 60,000 rupiah ($4.50) we go small harbor, big harbor, then back hotel."

Half an hour later, the menu had not changed much, but now he was only asking for 40,000. I wanted to walk and so I picked up the pace; so did he. I slowed down and he did the same. It was rather comical.

As we walked, we talked.

"How old are you?" I asked.

"I, 33."

"How old you mister?"

"73, but still can walk," and gave him a wink.

He laughed and wrinkles folded around his eyes.

"When I finish walking, I ride your beycha, but not today."

We were almost halfway to the market when I finally give in. I liked his casual style with none of the high-pressure sales pitch.

"OK, let's go," and I hopped in.

I learned a lot about this young man who had three young boys Chikal 10, Dirga 7, and the youngest, Akbar less than 50 days old. His wife was a 28-year-old Muslim. He was Catholic.

"What grade your boys?"

"They no go school, mister. Stay home. Cannot afford fifty-eight dollars a year for school."

"This beycha, I rent from Chinese man every day."

My ride today will pay him less than a fraction of his overhead.

So, I made this offer, "We go fish market. I buy your family a fish to eat."

"No mister, (smiling) fish too expensive, rice cheaper.

Rice can eat every day, cost me only 250,000 rupiahs one month (about $20)."

"How much does 'this' beycha cost?"

He replied with certainty, "500,000 rupiahs." The exchange rate made it out to be about thirty-nine dollars. The wheels were spinning both figuratively and literally as we made our way to the fish market. I was learning more than any guidebook riding with the Opihi Man. I was learning about the life of one person on this island of 19,000,000.

Upon reaching the small boat harbor, he told me, "These boats not for people...bring cement from Makassar and go New Guinea...bring rice and corn, no fishing. Fishing only small boat."

The boatmen he was pointing out were the famous Bugis who have been seafarers for centuries. They, like the Opihi Man, cannot afford to get sick nor have a holiday.

After our three-hour ride, I heard myself telling him: "Maybe, today your lucky day. Hari ini hari ke beruntungan."

"We go drink coffee now."

As of today, the Opihi Man is CEO and President in charge of his own company with a fleet of one very well-used beycha purchased for less than the price of a fake Rolex commonly sold on the streets of Bangkok.

Yes, hopefully, today can be a new start for the Opihi Man.

"Semoga sukses" Good Luck my friend."

"God bless, mister."

That's Earle, brother
Great Sunda Islands
Makassar, Sulawesi, Indonesia
2015

The Opihi Man of Makassar
(Two Years Later)

I wish that I could say that meeting the Opihi Man yesterday was the highlight of my return visit to Sulawesi, Indonesia, but it wasn't. If anything, it was the saddest part of any trip that I had taken recently.

I had met the Opihi Man at Fort Rotterdam in Makassar. I called him that because he clung to me like a Molokai Sea limpet until I relented and finally jumped into his beycha (a three-wheeled pedicab). That short ride established a two-year-old relationship and today, I finally returned to Makassar to try to find him again.

The major obstacle was finding a person whose name I did not know in the fourth largest city in Indonesia. Makassar has about 1.3 million inhabitants according to my friend Audy, the hotel manager.

But like in many other places, I started where I first met him at Fort Rotterdam, also known as Benteng Penyu or Sea Turtle Fort because of its shape. It was built in the 1670s by the Dutch as defense of their trade in the Celebes and was guarded fiercely against the Portuguese and other traders.

The makeup of Indonesia is complex, to say the least. While Indonesia is the largest Muslim country in the world,

Bali (maybe the most popular island in this 18,000-island archipelago) is entirely Hindu, while Flores Island, a thousand kilometers away, is Catholic; a testament to the Portuguese traders.

Sulawesi, has one Christian town, a dot on this island shaped much like a calligraphic "K," Tana Toraja is it. Anyone who is Protestant, speaks English, and lives anywhere on this island of 19 million can trace his roots back to Tana Toraja.

Upon returning to Fort Rotterdam, I started to show the Opihi man's photo to other beycha drivers, mostly men in their 50s and 60s. I had allowed only two days for my search in Sulawesi.

One driver stepped up and said, "That Yupi. I know Yupi." Yes, the Opihi man had a name.

Apparently, beycha drivers are a small minority in an industry quickly being swallowed up by motorized beychas, motorbike-driven beychas. And so, traditional beycha drivers tend to cluster together around Fort Rotterdam.

For 100,000 Indonesian Rupiah or $7.50, my beycha driver took me over bone-jarring roads, back toward the harbor and fish market, and into uncharted territory.

The farther we went, the deeper into the backstreets and neighborhoods he pedaled, the more astonished were the looks of residents. Children, like children everywhere, filled the air with laughter and giggles. While in the muddy, trash-littered streets, they called out, "hello" in English to me. Adults just stared in amazement, but we kept going.

Astonishingly, we came upon a place that my driver said, "this the house."

I had arrived uninvited, but was quickly welcomed into Yupi's home but not before taking off my shoes and entering a dark, dingy, unlit shack. It was there that I met Yupi, his wife, children, and parents.

The one-room house was bare-bones, spartan living with no toilet or running water and surrounded by open sewers and polluted canals so thick with rubbish that one could probably walk on water. Here was not just an impoverished family, but an entire neighborhood of tens of thousands of the poorest of poor who slept on bare floors or soiled mattresses in deplorable conditions.

My visit did not have the kind of reaction on me that I had envisioned. I thought that I would have been happy to see Yupi, but I wasn't. I was in a dilemma as I thought maybe Yupi was hitting the bottle and not working. After all, I dropped in on him to find him sleeping and his eyes blood-shot red. The usual doubts crept into my mind.

We hardly spoke to each other. It seems that he either didn't recognize me or in the presence of his father, had forgotten all his English. I spoke mainly with his dad who immediately pressed me for gifts and money. I wanted to get away as fast as I could and felt that maybe this was really just a big mistake on my part though I never felt threatened at any time, nor did I want to abandon Yupi.

I returned to my hotel. I felt like crap. The opulence of the hotel was like another world with air conditioning, marble floors, German Versus bathtub with hot and cold running water at my fingertips, a white, modern, porcelain Toto toilet, a king-sized bed, flat-screen TV, bathrobe, and matching slippers.

To think of where I had just been and to return to a palatial hotel was a bit too much. It was a miserably long and restless night, but I knew that I had to return to Fort Rotterdam the next day as I had promised Yupi that we would have a cup of coffee and talk business.

Sometimes, a time-out is in order. Getting away and maybe clearing the mind a bit then taking another look at the problem can be a good idea.

It came to me overnight. Why not try to hire a hotel worker on his day off to be my interpreter to accompany me to see Yupi. It would improve communications, answer some nagging questions and offer a second opinion from a local's perspective. Well, it turned out to be a great idea because that is how I met Audy, the day manager who happened to be off duty but at the hotel.

"Sure, Papi, I can do that."

Audy spoke excellent English and before meeting with Yupi, I gave him some background information.

"Audy, two years ago, I ran into Yupi. I liked him a lot and I thought he was an honest and humble man; a hard worker.

"When I found out that he rented his beycha for $16.00 a day, I bought it for him from the owner for $39.50. My hope was for him to be able to make some money for himself and maybe even send his sons to school."

"Be careful Papi. I worked in that area where the beycha drivers are. I know them well. Many are scammers, but we shall see."

Let's go see your friend."

It was 10:30 am when we showed up and met Yupi. He was there from 7:00 am in the morning.

Together, we entered the fort; grabbed some coffee; sat at a secluded table, and discussed business.

After a while, Audy shared this, "Papi, I am very impressed with Yupi. He is not like the others. He is an honest man."

I was greatly relieved to know that my initial trust in him was not misplaced.

"You know, with the beycha that you bought him, he was able to send one son to school.

"His wife also was able to buy an ice machine, so she makes home made snow cones and sells them to the neighbors.

"Now she is trying to save enough to start a small business making and selling food.

You could have knocked me over with a feather. A complete 180 degree turn around from yesterday has now put me over the moon. Not in my wildest dreams could I have imagined such events.

"OK, Audy, what does Yupi need? More beychas? Maybe buy a few more and rent them out?"

"No Papi, Yupi said that while the beychas are even cheaper now, he would not be able to find drivers as the young ones don't want to work that hard."

"He could use help in starting his wife out in a small food stand."

I was agreeable to that. "OK, then it's a done deal."

We continued to chat while sipping instant Kopi Luwak and shook hands on our agreement.

I told Yupi, "Yupi, your wife will be President of Yupi Enterprises. You can be the Vice President and I will be the Treasurer."

Audy chimed in, "Papi, I volunteer to be your site supervisor to check on Yupi's progress from time to time."

"Sounds good Audy. I thank you. You know none of this has happened without a reason. The three of us here are a part of our destiny."

"Papi, Yupi, and I have never met anyone like you. Yupi said that you are the first person to pay attention to him."

"Yupi was a stranger to me two years ago. Now, he is not only my business partner, but also my friend."

Yes, it was a good day at Yupi Enterprises.

That's Earle, brother
Makassar, Sulawesi
Greater Sunda Islands,
Indonesia
2017
More stories about Yupi to follow
www.ricetreechronicles.com

The Hanoi Breakfast Club

The Old Quarter of Hanoi offers travelers an amazing choice of small hotels like the Calypso and the Silver Legend. All are at bargain rates of about thirty dollars a night including breakfast.

At 7:30 in the morning, guests gather at the small hotel restaurant on the main floor. The price of lodging includes a quiet air-conditioned room and the friendliest staff of any hotel this side of the International Date Line. It is a great fit for me.

There was limited seating, four tables where strangers join strangers and soon become quick friends over a meal. English was the unifying language. One sits where there is an empty chair.

Today, a solitary Vietnamese girl dressed in school uniform and with an obvious disability to her left arm, joined me at the table. I guessed her age to be around eight. She was actually eleven. She sat alone at my table, and we ate in silence.

The following day, the same scenario was repeated, but now I knew her name, Pang.

That afternoon in the lobby, I met Ahn, a boy of nine. He wanted to practice his English with this stranger from

Hawaii. With the help of Hue, a 30% part-owner of the Silver Legend Hotel, he became animated. He joined me for breakfast the very next day. Pang also joined us. We were becoming a breakfast club.

To break the ice, I shared photos on my iPad. It was proving to be the single greatest social invention of the twenty-first century. Immediate, results somehow elicited the same response from young or old and across any language barrier or geographical frontier. Big smiles erupted when seeing themselves coming to life instantly on a big screen. 35mm camera screens didn't seem to have the same effect.

The hit attraction was a Christmas video of a standing toy moose dancing to the tune of Jose Feliciano's, "I want to wish you a Merry Christmas!" It swung to the left then to the right, each time getting closer to the edge of the coffee table, then finally falling off to the delight of the growing crowd. Smiles and giggles were the responses everywhere, and now we were suddenly six.

Then Pang surprised me and began to speak in English. She was really a seventh-grader in a rural village, an overnight train ride away. Through a Canadian benefactor, she had surgery for her broken arm.

We chatted about her school, and I heard myself promising to meet again in a few months at her village near Sapa, Vietnam. I wanted to visit Pang at her school.

Before leaving, Ahn and his parents also invited me to visit them in Ho Chi Min City. We were no longer strangers.

Suddenly, I felt rejuvenated. A destination and goal had been instantly established for maybe a future adventure?

After a month of traveling, I can't wait to get home yet, I can't help but feel a welling inside me to want to return.

The Hanoi Breakfast Club at the Silver Legend Hotel on Hang Bac Street in Hanoi was a great starting place, and fate would eventually reward me greatly.

That's Earle, brother
At the Silver Legend Hotel in The Old Quarter
Hanoi, Vietnam
2014

Sleuthing in Sapa with Bogie

As my gem hunting career is now on a semi-permanent hiatus, I have deemed the time appropriate to resurrect my sleuthing skills and focus on a new adventure.

I had grown up on the island of Maui in the forties, and fifties and Sunday nights at the King theater were movie nights for the family. Movies like the "Maltese Falcon" with Humphrey Bogart was a favorite. Bogie was the kind of guy that you'd want in your corner if you needed help. His tough-guy persona with cutting humor appealed to me. He was always at my side. I can still hear his familiar voice when I think of his character, Sam Spade, Private Eye.

It was only natural that I called on Bogie on this new adventure.

My challenge while on this trip to North Vietnam was to find and to meet up with previous acquaintances and to maintain my contacts and rekindle our friendship. I bore gifts of photographs and chocolate-covered macadamia nuts.

To a great extent, I did not have any difficulty meeting my former acquaintances; several were somewhat permanently established in storefronts or sidewalks in the Old Quarter of Hanoi.

My greatest challenge, however, was to find little Pang. She of the "Hanoi Breakfast Club" of last July. Some of you may recall this quiet, shy eleven-year-old village girl who was in Hanoi to get surgery for her arm.

She sat with me quietly three mornings for breakfast before finally speaking to me in perfectly clear English. I promised her that on my next trip, I would visit her in her village. Did I get her address? No, neither did I get her last name. I just knew that she was in a village outside of Sapa. I mean just how difficult would it be to find her.

I will dig deep like Humphrey Bogart as Private Eye Sam Spade in the Maltese Falcon and use my bag of tricks to find her.

I can hear it now. Bogie would have said, "We'll find you precious. Yes, I want to see that pretty face again. Yes, even if it takes me 20 years, I'll find you, and if I don't, well, at least I will always remember you."

Well, after a nine-hour trip by train and bus, I arrived in Sapa to search for little Pang. But where to start?

A large wall map in the hotel lobby showed the nearby villages, all twenty-six of them. I had three days to find her.

But first things first. I showered, shaved, brushed my teeth, and...hello! What's this across the street, next to the Nha Nghi Viet Duc Guest House? A North Face Outlet Store, tiny, but the red sign was hypnotizing. I was drawn to it like a zombie.

Well, ten minutes and three jackets later and I was ready for some serious sleuthing. Shopping can have unexpected results, really.

While at the shop, Haa the owner, told me she could rent me a room and motorbike; wash and dry my clothes; cut and dry my hair; polish my shoes; give me a manicure and pedicure; clothe me and feed me at her coffee house. She was a one-woman conglomerate.

We chatted, and I shared what my mission was. She said, "maybe I can help." She ran across the street to call two Hmong ladies to come over and to look at two photos I had with me, maybe they knew her. Yes, fat chance of that happening; they looked, but there was no joy in Coopers Town that night. I struck out.

Meanwhile, back at the hotel, my room wasn't quite ready and the desk clerk listened to my story. "Let me talk to your 30% owner of the Silver Legend Hotel in Hanoi, maybe she can help."

Yes, maybe Hue can help. We chatted by phone and LINE. She had the phone number of someone from the same village as Pang, except no one knew which of the twenty-six villages she was from. No one answered the phone. It may have been a dead end as the terrain was mountainous, and many people had no phones.

Eventually, the seamstress across the street picked up on my exploits. She too offered to help. It was getting more intriguing by the hour, and my support group grew to about ten ladies. Finally, after passing Pang's picture around, came a voice saying... "I know this girl!" What were the chances of this happening anywhere?

"I think she from Lao Chai village," then quickly, she disappeared behind a building only to reappear with two other Hmong women who happened to be from the same village. Both scrutinized the photos. "Yes, this one," pointing not to Pang, but to someone else in a second photo.

"She from Lao Chai village."

"Yes, yes (now pointing to Pang's photo) I know this girl mother, father die, mother working." Still, another grabbed a phone and punched in some numbers.

"Her mother is leading a trek now, but she will come to see you at three today."

I was stunned. Fully, a dozen strangers have accomplished what I might never have done in a month of Sundays.

My new career as a sleuth replete with Stetson, dressed in black and doing a bad Bogie impression was coming together. Maybe, just maybe, I had some potential here in Sapa as a private investigator. Hmmmm.

I could just hear Bogie, "You done good kid. You may not make it today, maybe not tomorrow, but you will make it as a gumshoe someday."

"Yes Bogie, this could be the start of a wonderful friendship."

That's Earle brother
Sleuthing in Sapa, Vietnam
2014

https://www.ricetreechronicles.com

The Twinkle in Maura's Eyes

I first met Maura through a friend of a friend. She had advertised her service as an English-Spanish-French speaking guide. I thought it would be a great way to get my bearings in Havana and maybe be lucky enough to get an insight into one person's life growing up in Cuba.

This is her story.

I was fifteen years old and remember leaving late one night. "Come on…you and your brothers must get ready. Take everything and let's go" was her mother's soft, but commanding voice. She was a woman of great inner strength, but of few words.

"Con prisa chiquitos, vamanos."

It was nearly a full Harvest moon when Maura, her mother, and her two younger brothers walked out of a house in the middle of the night balancing their belongings on their heads, and returned to the forest of Pino del Rio.

The path leading to the flat wooded area, which when cleared was ideal for planting tobacco, held no clue for Maura. All she knew was that she trusted her mother, for it was from her mother's milk that she nurtured her dream and fierce independence that firmly grounded her to this land.

A single mother with three mouths to feed and alone with no man, they had no money at all, but at least, they had a home.

In the dark, Maura could see the full moon through a hole in the thatched roof as well as the grass growing a foot tall through the cracks in the sandy clay floor still, it was a shelter for the three which her mother had built single-handedly years before.

Snuggling together to preserve warmth, sleep came slowly as they were to spend the first of many nights on the bare, earthen floor.

Maura thought, "What chance do I have as the daughter of a poor campesina? The other kids will make fun of me. They will laugh at my tattered clothes. I don't look like the others even though we are all poor. I know that we will somehow be looked upon as lower than anyone else."

"Do not worry 'mi amor', I will make your clothes," cooed my mother and she did. And shoes as well. My mother somehow even made me a pair of shoes.

"But we have no money," I said.

"We have no money today, Maura, but tomorrow is another day." My mother was like that, reassuring and quietly confident, and maybe that is why I am such an optimist.

Here was this resourceful woman, daughter of multiple generations of compesinos, who had only a few years of primary education herself, but who knew instinctively that education would be the vehicle to a better life in her country.

It was as though she foresaw the future when the federal government outlined a national priority consisting of the

Five National Endeavors: Education, Health, Sports, Arts, and Culture.

My mother was a proud woman who always told me that education would be my salvation, that I should always study, always and that it was my responsibility to make a difference in my life. It was not a matter of trying, but doing.

To this day, it is like a recording in my mind and as my mother predicted, it was through continuing my studies and multiple backup plans in case plan A, B…or Z failed to materialize that I always knew I would create my own options.

My mother was like that and so am I. I knew somehow that I would make a difference in my life, but at fifteen, one doesn't have all the answers, especially someone who came from nothing and still had nothing except for the clothes that she carried in a bundle.

When I look back at my life, I am proud of what I have accomplished. Today, I have a life where caring for my mother and little brother is a given, but it was not an easy path to follow.

I spent ten lonely years after my husband, and I parted. I learned English; raised a son; worked in the tobacco curing barns, and taught since I was 18; went to the University and got my degree in journalism; worked for news agencies and knitted clothing when my son needed it. I didn't have one job with long hours; I had many jobs with long hours. It is the way that we live here in Cuba, we must. But I was able to build a small home by myself, just as my mother had done. It is where she and my brother live just outside the capital, near Guanajay.

Today, I am happily married to Geraldo, and our plan is for us to save for an apartment in the city.

So now, I work as a journalist for both television and newspapers, teach English and Spanish, give classes in a private school, hire myself out as an English, Spanish or French speaking personal guide for private clients, and occasionally write articles for publication.

I have a dream, but even that was elusive twenty years ago. Much is changing in our country with the five expanded initiatives: The ability to travel abroad; the encouragement of starting small businesses; the luring of foreign investments; the buying and selling of private property and the promotion of tourism.

Young people have dreams, something unimaginable when we were growing up. Innovative entrepreneurs are choosing to stay and open businesses like Jacqueline whose coffee shop and combined clothing gallery are on the cusp of the cutting edge of change and could compete in Los Angeles or New York.

Oh, the future is starting to look bright here. You can see the quick pace of restoration projects of the most spectacular colonial limestone architecture in all of Spanish-speaking America. The excitement is almost palpable.

A speeding train of change is on the way. Tourism is growing even more rapidly than two years ago. The populace and government may or may not be ready for change, but it will come.

The confidence that an open-door policy will bring about a tangible dream for all, rests with people like Maura, young,   educated,   articulate,   enthusiastic,   talented, determined, and yet never abdicating her campesino roots.

She lives the dream, and it is on her shoulder, and of others like her, that will determine Cuba's future success. Quite frankly, I have no doubt that the country will be in good hands.

There certainly is a ray of sunshine coming from the Caribbean, and that beacon of optimism and hope comes from the twinkle in Maura's eyes.

That's Earle, brother
Havana, Cuba
2014

The Walnut Man

Before leaving Cacabellos, I spent time with hotel owner Sr. Luis.

"Tomorrow will be a long uphill climb, my friend. I walk about 6–7 miles every day for exercise."

"Papi, you and I are the same age. I suggest you walk to Trabadero only and rest there overnight before pushing on to Cebreiro."

I have come to place much emphasis on talking and listening to locals in the area not just because they sometimes seem so lost in private thoughts and that makes me curious, but more because it is an enjoyable thing to do. Seniors are a wealth of knowledge and besides, they often share great wisdom through their stories.

I remember my counselor friend from Wahiawa, Hawaii who always asked, which of your five senses is most important?

"It is the power of the ear" was his reply. Ralph was right. As I visit each place in my journeys, it has always been the ability to listen to what people were saying that has proven most rewarding.

Whether in Old Havana with Maura who openly spoke about life in Havana in harsh and realistic tones not found in magazine articles, or with the young apprentice monk in Luang Prabang on the Mekong River sharing his desire to be educated. It was what they said, which was more important than anything I could have revealed to them even if I had tried.

And so as I meandered along the Camino, I have learned to walk slower and listen to people along the way. This practice has made all the difference in my adventures.

It is not the packaged tours to the Mayan ruins, not the awe of Macchu Picchu, not the overpowering ruins at Angkor Wat, nor the chicken skin feeling of the "Killing Fields" near Battambang, Cambodia, nor to the other great destinations of the world that interest me. My bucket list is not a container for future goals, but I fill it up with whomever I meet along the way.

And so, today has proven to be like many of my best days. It was not the destination, but the people. This is how I met the Walnut Man.

As I made my way uphill through thirteen miles of back roads, I saw a man walking toward me with his dog. A casual hello turned into an hour's chat.

"Buenas Tardes Señor. How are you today?"

"I am fine, thank you."

He had something in his hand, and I thought I'd ask.

"Señor, what is that?"

I had seen this shell before and thought that I might already know his answer. It might have been a chestnut, but the ones on the road were immature and held no history.

"Well, these are chestnuts, but this year has been a bad year. Too Dry for the nuts to develop and to grow to maturity.

"See these young ones, nothing inside. Not enough rain."

"So these trees here are chestnut trees? I have never seen them before. I only see chestnuts in the markets, never having picked them off the ground as you are doing now."

"Do you live here?"

"Yes, my wife is from Trabadero, and much of her family is here. I was born not far from here, but we live in Barcelona. Still, we come here for the coolness and tranquility especially when it is hot in Barcelona.

"See those big trees over there. They are walnuts. I am 74 years old, but those trees are over 800 years old. But what do you think is happening?"

"Young people want to make quick money and not think about the future. If you cut this tree down, you will never see another like it. Look around you, it brings tears to my eyes."

I spied cut timber twenty feet high alongside the road. He wept for the fallen giants.

"I think trees are living things and of such elegance that they should be preserved for all mankind. Ahh, if only I could hear the stories of those Pilgrims who rested under their shade or stopped to admire their beauty."

"These trees are on my property and must be cared for. You cannot plant them. They just grow, but the underbrush must be cleared for the trees to be healthy. See under the trees here? I cleared all of that yesterday."

"Here, look at these," and he scooped up a few walnuts.

"Aaah," as if holding a precious gem, "here is a good one, but once you crack it open, you must peel off the skin, otherwise it is bitter."

"This one here, this smaller one is sweeter and of a different variety. You can eat this one without peeling off the inner layer of skin."

He was a delight to listen to, and his unbridled love and devotion for the walnut tree brought great joy to me.

"You know, señor, there may be few who share this love for the walnut trees as much as you do," I said, "but I can tell you that I feel very privileged to be in your company today."

"I thank you Papi."

"Vaya con Dios, señor."

I think these trees will be in good hands. For now, they are safe with the Walnut man.

That's Earle, brother
Trabadero, Spain
2016

Them...

The northern frontier city of Chiang Mai, Thailand is being invaded. From across the borders they come, multi-generational hordes carving their way through teak forested mountains and into the lowlands of the Ping River Valley, where the numerous waterways laced with emerald green rice fields are their desired destination. They are everywhere and multiplying more and more as time goes on. Little did I realize, but I would come face to face with "Them" this evening on the streets of Nimanhaemin.

Nimanhaemin was the earliest Chiang Mai family in this northern city of Thailand not far from Burma and Laos. This area is now considered Chiang Mai's hotspot and the hippest place dotted with restaurants, coffee shops, book stores, and spas.

Upon my arrival to Chiang Mai last evening, I decided to reconnoiter my surroundings. I was unaware. I was in unfamiliar territory. An evening stroll would be my first adventure and conjuring up sage advice from the back pages of Gunji's Manual, I knew that when in a strange place, walk in a straight line, turn left, keep walking and keep making only left turns. If done correctly, one should end up back where one started, but more on that later. It was getting dark, and my destination was Nimanhaemin Road, but all that I could see was a long dark highway with no sidewalks.

Well, when in a strange place, ask a local, and so I did. My basic Thai, however, never included "Help, I am lost. Where is Nimanhaemin Road?" Fortunately, the security guard pointed "in that direction," and that is where I headed toward a full moon rising under a hazy night sky. In the far-off distance, I could make out lights flickering through the canopy of trees, there were a few buildings nestled among food stands alongside empty fields.

It seemed longer, but after hugging the pedestrian pathway while avoiding being night roadkill, I could see movement, heavy with speeding two and four-wheeled vehicles.

I turned left on Niman Road, the local's version of this rather long non Thai-sounding name, where the lighted street offered a multi-colored, brightly lit menu of restaurants, shops, businesses, and spas as far as one could see.

I perceived no visible threats of any kind save for having to walk on the streets as the sidewalks were a course in pedestrian steeplechase with uneven, sloping, or even totally blocked off paths. The only safe place to walk seemed to be on the street dealing with two-wheeled, motorized terror.

I eventually stopped by Sabai Sang Spa…my nails were in bad need of attention, and like with any visitor to Thailand,–there is eating and there are manicures. Well, I could always eat later. I opted for the pedicure and manicure combo.

A friendly, chubby lady greeted me with the magic words…"having air conditioning." I already love this place.

First lady: "We busy, busy now. Have many Chinese tourists, more than Australian more than Falang" (Most commonly describing Americans and Europeans). Much of the influx has been attributed to a highly successful Chinese movie released in 2012 called, "Lost in Thailand" which was filmed mainly in Chiang Mai. Over a million visitors from China have already passed through Chiang Mai in the first five months of 2015.

First lady: "Where you from Mr.?"

"From Hawaii…"

First lady: "Oh Hawaii very buchiifu…I see in books, ha ha."

Her eyes twinkled as she spoke.

As we chatted, a young, tall, slender, well-tanned lady with broad shoulders and a beguiling smile began to wash and massage my feet. Oh, did I mention, I got the entire package…manicure and pedicure with foot massage for 700 baht or $19 at today's exchange rate.

The first lady kept chatting away, talking to my nails mostly, and began her work in earnest.

"OK, OK?" she showed me the results of my index finger. "Short, OK?"

"No short. Nid noi (little bit)…no short."

A typical manicurist here will cut your nails down to the quick and file it down even more. My lady was totally focused and seemed intent on achieving nothing less than nail annihilation. It didn't matter what I asked for, there would only be one length to fit all…very close to the bone.

I felt more like a victim than a customer as she ignored my pleas of "Jep, jep" (pain) while attempting to pull my fingers away. It was only after crying "Mae" (mother in Thai) that she paused, looked up from her work, her eyes laughing, smiled, and then continued to grind my nails down to the quick.

The lady working my feet seemed more intuitive. She seemed to know the moment I was in pain and whispered softly to lady number one, but the occasional torture never ceased.

I, still totally enjoyed my manicurist, after all, when she made you laugh so much, you didn't feel the pain.

First lady: "Chinese not like manicure-pedicure...only like foot and oil massage...so many Chinese. Can speak Chinese little, English little bit..." as in only a little bit of nail left on my fingers, a thought which crossed my mind.

Meanwhile, the young lady working my feet didn't say much, but her strong hands felt good on my tired soles. Hmmm, she sure had strength in her fingers and applied even more pressure when I said, "I like sa-trong (sic) my feet."

Aaaah, this was great...when suddenly, she bolted upright and slapped something in midair "Ha ha, I get them!" Wow, she was not only strong and toned but had quick, cat like reflexes. She opened her palms and pulled off a tiny dot of a mosquito.

First lady..."Them, many, many." Door open, door close...many, many mosquitos," as lady number two again slapped the air and smiling, produced another blood-stained victim.

I am now getting the picture, "them" are mosquitos. In fact, a shop that I visited, on the way here, displayed colorful incense coils aka mosquito repellent, bottled coconut oils for mosquito bites, and soothing lavender lotions to treat the welts. Everyone sold the stuff…it was a clue.

Have I stumbled onto the mosquito capital of Thailand? I have met "Them" first hand and well, squashing them one at a time is something the local Lanna (traditional northern province people) know how to do well.

The evening ended with a warm cup of tea and an invitation to return, but at the way my nails looked, I don't think I'll be back for at least a fourth night.

Out on Niman Road again, I made my way looking for more left turns and a long, long walk home.

Addressing a driver, I asked…" mister, you know Chomdoi two building. 'bai baan' (go home), I want find my room."

Songtel (Chiang Mai commuter truck taxi) driver: "Chai khrap, Mai pen rai (not a problem) only twenty baht."

And so I took a Songtel safely back home without testing Gunji's theory about making consecutive left turns. I am sure he was correct.

It was a good evening. I met "Them" and I got my nails trimmed at the same time…all in all, a great night.

That's Earle, brother
Chiang Mai, Thailand
2016

Today They Shall Eat Ice Cream

Ever since seeing Bing Crosby, Bob Hope, and Dorothy Lamour in "The Road to Bali" which was produced in 1952, I have longed for exotic places even though most "Road" movies were shot in the backlots of Hollywood studios. The "Road to Bali" was the sixth of seven movies and the only one to be shot in Technicolor.

Their movies are as entertaining today as when they were first produced and show the great chemistry between Crosby and Hope. I never knew where in the world Bali was, but it has always beckoned to me.

And so, it is understandable that I have again returned to Bali, but to one quite a bit different than the movie.

Walking the streets of Kuta, in Denpasar, Bali is like playing a game of dodgeball. Pedestrians are at constant threat of being run down by racing motorbikes that careen off narrow streets with no shoulders. Frequently, two cars face stand-offs where one has to back down and reverse down narrow winding streets.

The motorbike "mafia" is probably the most disagreeable bunch as they try to get your attention by grabbing your arm from their territorial corners. Honking taxi drivers troll for your business. Shop owners are less aggressive, though not by much.

Bars and convenience stores like Circle K and Coco Mart have sprouted up like weeds and dominate the landscape. Now, it also seems that every third shop has become a Spa. Bali has changed, but still, if one looks hard enough, there are wonderful people to meet. After all, Bali's attractions are her people.

It is like most other places in the world, people make the difference.

My friends, Ifun and Paskal, the ones who coined my name "Papi," from the island of Flores, are such a couple. I visited with them yesterday and brought some chocolate-covered Macadamia nuts from home. Hugs and the excitement from both made it all worthwhile. Next year, I will hopefully be able to drag Ms. Carolina for a return trip to Indonesia and go by motorbike to a city near their village on Flores Island where there is a school for the blind.

You know this custom of Hawaii locals bringing gifts with them when visiting friends has paid off tenfold. Whether it may be photos that I took the previous trip, chocolates, or even an inexpensive watch from Longs Drugs, they are overcome with joy that you even stopped by to say hello, a gift in hand or not.

Today, while walking down another nondescript side street, I came upon one of the scores of massage spas. This one looked no different than most, although there was a smiling face from inside the window. I didn't feel like I was being solicited like so many other places where street hawkers pull you by the shirt sleeves and practically drag you into their shops.

I went in and met Penny, a Balinese native of about 35.

"Hello, Papi! Come in!"

At first, I was astonished by this greeting. "How did you know my name?" I thought.

Oh, I guess they call all mature men, "Papi", meaning "Father."

Penny had a Balinese smile to welcome all sunbaked travelers. Recognizing her beauty was immediate, then I noticed her limp.

She caught me looking.

"Oh, when I was six years old, I got Polio and couldn't walk for five years.

"But my three children are all healthy, and I am happy for that."

She smiled and was open and sharing of her story. I continued to listen.

I then asked, "Penny, how is business in Bali?"

"Oh Papi, it is noon, and you are only our first customer."

"Sometimes, we don't have any."

"Yes, I've passed dozens of massage spas and nearly all appeared completely empty. Totally void of customers."

It stands to reasons why owners of small businesses had been so aggressive on the streets. Business has been dismal and this was the pre-pandemic days.

"Penny, are you the owner of this shop?"

"No Papi. I am just a worker here. I work here every day. No day off."

"That would not happen in my country."

Sadly, though, it happens regularly in many Southeast Asian countries.

"Penny. I noticed that an hour foot massage is only about 80,000 Indonesian Rupiah, about $5.98."

"That is really cheap."

I am curious as to how she will reply to my next question.

"You massage one hour. How much does your boss pay you?"

I know most spa workers are paid by commission and not hourly.

"My boss Australian man. He pay me 10%."

"You mean for one hour; you get only 8,000 rupees?"

"Yes, Papi."

My phone shows the exchange rate. Penny made all of 60 cents by me.

I was astounded. "How can eat?"

"I only eat one cup of noodles a day.

"Every day, I give my two oldest children 5,000 Rupee for lunch."

"That's 37 cents a day for two!"

"Yes, we have no money, but my husband and I work every day so our family can eat.

"My son wants a phone, but I say we cannot afford one. We cannot even afford anything special like an ice cream for them."

I feel my composure abandoning me.

I do what has now become a habit.

"Penny, you and your family are healthy and are together. It is Sunday.

Today they will eat ice cream."

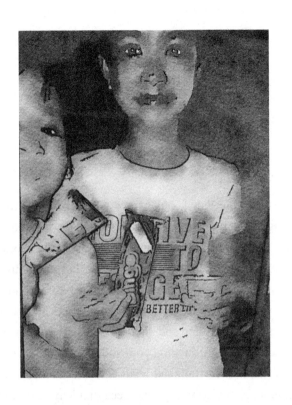

That's Earle, brother
Bali, Indonesia
2017
https://www.ricetreechronicles.com

Trekking Borneo

It was not quite dawn, but I have taken the steps toward walking across a restricted bridge and into the low land rain forest of Balikpapan, Kalimantan (Borneo) about 40 kilometers from the city, where nothing but unidentifiable whirring sounds; movement in the bushes around me; distant primates calling out to their neighbors; strange birds suddenly taking flight and the ever-present sound of the soft, wet, loamy soil sucking your shoes back into its tracks.

The unmarked trailhead leads into the thickest part of the jungle, over rotting logs and decaying leaves, definitely a trail seldom used.

There was no one else around me. The area was deserted at this hour, but with the help of my driver, we have found a fairly virgin section of the low-land rain forest. My driver soon left me, and I was alone.

There were signs that people may have been here at one time, and surely someone will eventually follow in my footsteps, but for now, I was the very first going where no sane man should be venturing alone at this time of the day in the jungle.

I had been told that it is not safe. While there were no really major predators, legends persisted that giant snakes caused the disappearance of several village children along the Burak river, but this was many, many years ago.

Borneo has no tigers like Sumatra and the threat from the Honey Bears of Borneo (Helactos malayanus euryspilus) and the Bornean orangutans are minimal, at least in this part of the rainforest.

As I ventured deeper down into the ravines, I found myself constantly looking back for self-assurance that I would be able to return to my starting point without the assistance of the special search, and rescue team that is on constant 24/7 alert in Balikpapan.

At times, the jungle opened up to reveal beams of sunlight through the thick canopy of leaves and just as quickly, turned into darkness with only the sounds of a symphony of cicadas hidden among the trunks of the jungle giants.

There was something among the brushes ahead and to the left of me, but before I could get a look at it, whatever it was, only the leaves trembling in its wake were visible. My heart jumped a beat, but panic was the last thing to do in the jungle. I knew not to run, but my steps now became more deliberate.

I was constantly looking in the upper reaches of the canopy fully expecting to see "him," the person of the forest translated from Bahasa Indonesia as "orang" (person) "hutan" (forest).

Days before, I was warned by two people. "When you see him, be quiet. He seldom makes sounds unless mating, but he will be shaking the trees to make his presence known. Do not cause him stress."

"Yes, I know," and smiled at the women. I knew what they meant. If stressed, orangutans have been known to give you a "golden shower" to tell you a thing or two.

So, I was cautious, but would not be surprised if there was to be a sudden "sprinkle" from above. I pressed on, but the mosquitoes were relentless, and the exposed parts of my body quickly appeared as hundreds of angry red pimples. There was no stopping. The only direction was forward.

Imagination can really play mind games and so far, I was no exception. I envisioned myself being carried off by millions of inch-long carnivorous red ants; clawed by giant river otters and having my blood sucked out of me by the large bats hanging overhead.

Where was I? Which path leads back to the trailhead? I was getting nervous and heard my heart thumping in the back of my head. I sensed an uneasiness, and something or someone was quickly approaching me.

"Ticket, sir, your ticket, sir."

"The jungle ride is over."

"You may get out now."

"We hope you enjoyed your ride at Balikpapan nature park. It's not often we get single adults riding the children's trolley."

That's Earle, brother
Trekking Borneo's Rainforest
Balikpapan, Kalimantan/Borneo, Indonesia
Greater Sunda Islands
2015

Would You Send Your Child to School in These?

A cloud of fumigated smoke turned the morning dark for a few minutes as I took refuge from the vector control unit. "Yes, señor, we have a mosquito problem. No Malaria, but we have Dengue." It was an opening to start a conversation.

I was standing next to two men who invited me inside their home to sit.

"The bearded one...he is old...he will be gone soon."

It was the first reference to Castro that I've heard spoken aloud. "His name" had never arisen in any previous conversation with anyone on the island.

Javier and Abelardo (not their real names) were openly discontented, but not angry. Having a foreign ear to address opened them up a bit.

"How can we live? Yes, up the street by the church is nicer, that is because of tourism, but for us, life goes on without much change. We are the neglected."

"Look at us, my sister and I live here. I have three children. My boy is away at school most of the time as he is a boxer."

"Maybe one day, the next Teofilo Stevenson," I replied with a smile. They all laughed. "Yes, that would be great."

"My other boy lives with my brother because we have no room here."

He failed to mention the third child.

Coro (not her real name), his sister, shared the one-room, ground-floor apartment with a single piece of furniture and a double bed along with two chickens and a handful of chicks. She herded them protectively into the living space and had accounted for each one as we talked.

"See, this is my house, but I have nothing."

Abelardo openly allowed me to look. Barebones, dark, no lights, no screen windows, a double burner for cooking, a kerosene lamp, and a scattered eclectic collection of religious artifacts. I saw no bathroom nor did I ask.

"You are lucky; all your education is free."

"Yes," added Abelardo, "but you need a backpack, school supplies, and shoes all of which you pay on your own. Here, here are my son's shoes. Would you send your child to school in these?"

He held up a shoe with a hole the size of a silver dollar. Its appearance was like the sun-bleached flotsam that you would find washed up on a beach. "It costs $3.00 which I cannot afford." He shared his plight but had not asked me for any money.

They knew about Hawaii and the Hula dancers, but it was mostly the hard economic realities that concerned them. It was living day-by-day by the seat of their pants.

Journalists, housewives, university students, hotel workers, grandparents, teachers, barbers, or doctors all seemed to have one thing in common. It was not hunger as I had surmised on a previous trip, but how to live once the hunger had been satisfied somewhat. The everyday necessities were very real, but now they are looking forward to a bit more.

There was daily drama playing out in front me. A woman sat crying uncontrollably as her companion left, only to return to comfort her. A man walking his Akita seemingly without a care and school kids carrying heavily laden backpacks scurried off, already late for classes. Fifty-something-year-old Chevys, Pontiacs, Dodges, Cadillacs, and a few Russian Hugos sped in all directions with apparent missions ahead.

Faces, like the facades of old buildings, reflected decades of struggle. People aged quickly here. One does when there is precious little to eat and multiple mouths to feed; when jobs pay so meagerly that one must be creatively seeking other sources of income.

Abelardo, who held up his son's shoes as if to make a statement to the outside world, lacked life's basic necessities and modern conveniences. What they lacked, they make up by looking for other ways to make do. It is a national trait.

That's Earle, brother
Havana, Cuba
2014

El Norte

It has been seven long years since Elena broke her wrist; since I left the cold three blanket nights of Quetzaltenango, in the Western Highlands of Guatemala for the likes of Isleta de Gaia; since the altitude burnt a hole in my chest and the cobblestone streets ate the soles of my shoes; and since I realized that I was not capable of pulling even one more cylinder of propane gas up the street on a hand cart. It was then that I gave up and fled to the shore.

In 2008, Elena was a 38-year-old recent widow, with two school-aged children who had barely completed primary school. Somehow, she raised them and carried on her husband's propane gas business. In the mountainous Quetzaltenango region with its cobblestone streets built on hills, it was no easy task pulling a hand cart ladened with propane cylinders up and down the streets of Xela, a name most locals use about Quetzaltenango.

I lived with Elena and her family for several weeks by renting a room and sharing a single bathroom in fifteen minutes shifts in the morning rush to work or school. Others were there, notably Spanish language students from Thailand and the U.S. That was several years ago, and now

I was returning to see how my adopted Guatemalan family was doing.

My taxi searched the streets below the park without success. I knew that Elena's place was close by. My planned visit to see her and her family, however spontaneous, might not work out after all. There was no way to contact her by phone.

"The entire family may have moved, señor. It's been known to happen. They go North, señor."

It's quite easy to give up, but I came five thousand miles to see my Guatemalan family, and I wasn't giving up this easily. Thoughts of a cold, wet night alone in a Gothic like cathedral of a hotel made me shiver.

Quetzaltenango is near the Mexican border. Only in recent history has there been peace and a pause in the killing of thousands of indigenous Guatemaltecos by the military. Today, it is considered a safe haven compared to Guatemala City, but it is light years away from modernization.

After stopping by a small shop that I knew, I was given directions to Elena's home. We have reunited once again.

It was remarkable to see how Elena managed all these years alone. She had been to the U.S. to seek work as a domestic. In the process, she had to leave her small family to fend for themselves. Jarvis, now 25, had finished college but was still unemployed. Yuselfi, then a high school student was now a single parent of a very bright and articulate two-year-old.

They owned a car and motorbike housed in their indoor garage. Signs of her stay in the U.S were evident; it was the emotional scars that I would learn about later that remained hidden.

We talked into the night. She shared her treatment by her employers, the 12–16-hour days working in Beverly Hills and Las Vegas mansions, and the loneliness of being away from her children. Between jobs, she sold oranges on the streets of Wilshire Boulevard. The crowding into shared shelters for the night and the solitude were all a sacrifice for her family. It was not easy, she told her kids over a dinner of plain spaghetti and wieners with a few corn tortillas, but if the opportunity came up again, "I would go. We will go North."

"Sometimes, when I had no money, I'd eat a donkey." The surprise on my face was obvious until she added, "You know, a little burro. I'd eat nothing, but a burrito." She has never lost sight of that bit of humor that has helped her to go on.

Listening to her into the late hours of the night, I realized that Elena's story was just another chapter in the lives of women all over the world. Women like Mai in Hanoi and Mighty Moe in Sapa make unimaginable personal sacrifices to support their families. They are all pages in a book that may get written; it's just that Elena has already lived through several volumes of her own story.

It is a never-ending struggle which reads like Sisyphus pushing a boulder up the hill only to have it roll back down again. The characters are real and their challenges ceaseless. Will it never end? God, I sure hope it does. If not in my lifetime, maybe theirs.

That's Earle, brother
Quetzaltenango, Guatemala
2014

The Albeeno Aborigine

While at the Chiang Rai Night Bazaar in northern Thailand and looking for an empty seat to enjoy my meal, a smiling face greeted me.

"Have a seat mate. Anyone can sit hea. Me name's Staive," extending an open hand, "I'm an Albeeno Aborigine."

The initial look on my face revealed a puzzlement.

Quick, think, think.

"Oh, you mean an albino aborigine."

"Yes, mate, that's what I am." He let out a friendly laugh.

And so a casual walk, through the night bazaar looking for a place to have a meal, turned into a rather interesting evening with this relatively new, two-week-old Aussie expat from Victoria.

With a hot bowl of stew, I asked the stranger if anyone could sit at the surrounding tables.

"Pull up a chair, mate. Join me." And so I did.

His name was "Staive", Steve to most of you. An ex-school bus driver who was four years my junior and had relocated to Chiang Rai for a new experience; a chance at life and a new beginning.

"You know me mate's wife has a friend. Nice lady, Tum, with a daughter and two sons. She had a rough life and all. Got badly treated by her ex-husband and then he took off. She's well educated, knows a good bit of English and can read and write as well."

"I'm to meet her on Friday. She's driving all the way from Mae Chan by motorbike. That's a good bit of haulin."

"I should know, mate, I drove a rural school bus for ten 'ears'. You know the kids all loved me. They didn't want me to leave but I said I gotta go."

"Even me former riders have an occasional 'bia' with me and greet me regularly. Guess I am a bit loved, you know."

"Well, Steve, must be your great attitude and Santa Claus beard."

He stroked his beard which was finely trimmed and framed his rosy cheeks.

I would be nursing a beer for over an hour as I didn't think I could sit with an Aussie and drink a Pepsi. Something about that just didn't sound right.

"Yeeah, Papi, I've been coming hea about three times now. I was in Chiang Mai, then heard about Chiang Rai so I hopped on a bus and here I am. You know, when I got off the bus, I knew."

I nodded.

"Yes, me too Steve. The pace is several notches below that of Chiang Mai, and it is a very walkable city. I love it here."

"Yes, I just picked up a truck. Amazing experience. I don't speak Thai but had to buy two tires. Went to a tire shop and talked with a couple of blokes. After an hour, I came away with two new tires. I ask em', how much for putting 'em on and balancing them…100 baht? What? It's like 3.70 Australian you know."

"So I says OK, you fix my GPS and camera and set it up on the dashboard…bam, bam, bam and two hours later…how much? 100 baht I say, no no, I give you 200 baht, and I almost had to force it on them."

"I like the Thai people. You know, you give them respect and they give it back 10-fold to you."

Those words had a familiar ring to it.

"Yesterday, I walked from me pad to hea and must have had a 100 people smile at me."

"Yes, a smile goes a long way here."

"I think that I simply get what I want by smiling and pointing a finger at what I want. A smiling simpleton is what I am…ha ha."

Steve was such a likable fellow that it was easy to see how people gravitated to him.

"Yes, that's all it takes. The Thais are wonderful people."

"When I left Victoria, I packed just two bags and hea I am."

"I am already looking into a house. I'll be happy to take care of the lady, her kids, one who is a bit slow in the head, and her elderly mother. Yes, a bloke's gotta do these things for a Thai wife."

"I don't mind. It makes me happy."

He reminded me of Erik the Red. He was the retired DEA law enforcement officer who kept going back to his laundry lady twice a day for the past year and asking her if she was ready to be his girlfriend and that he would build a house for her two kids and elderly mother so they wouldn't have to sleep on the floor of the laundry shop.

Well, I never did see Eric on my recent visit, but here was another guy with a kind heart who was happy to do the same thing. I hope that they both succeed. It seems that happiness is within arm's reach, and they are willing to reach out.

You occasionally meet guys like Steve and Eric, both of whom were wonderfully pleasant and open. I liked both of them instantly.

My only problem was understanding what Steve was trying to tell me.

He addressed that. "Yeah, you know we Aussies speak too fast and with our mouths closed. The Thais can't understand a word I'm saying, but I will learn to speak Thai. I heard that Tum is a great teacher. Speaking a bit of Thai will be a plus."

Yes, Steve, I second that.

"It will be great to meet up with you again. Just let me pay for the beer."

"No Papi, this is my share. You know what we Aussies mean by my share?"

"When we have a drink, one person pays for the first round...that's his share. After a second round of drinks, you pay, that's your share."

"OK, if you insist mate. Tomorrow will be my share."

That's Earle, brother

Chiang Rai Night Bazaar

Chiang Rai, Thailand

2016

https://www.ricetreechronicles.com

The Road to Rio

Rio de Janeiro is probably the most famous of all Brasilian cities, but the "Road to Rio" covers cities from Manaus in the Amazon to Rio Grande do Sul in the South. Brasil is geographically larger than the contiguous U.S.

He No-Look Too Good

Fellow Peace Corps buddy Steve just shared an article that his mom had clipped out of a newspaper in 1969. Here is the brief article in its entirety..." Jose the Salesman. Belo Horizonte, Brazil-(AP). Police arrested Jose Cassiano De Jesus yesterday for selling lots on the moon at $24 each. Jose told potential clients he sold the first lot to Neil Armstrong and that Armstrong had gone to the moon to inspect his property.

That story conjured up a few old memories both about super salesmen, con artists, and typical small-town dealings in and around the Zona da Cana in northeastern Brazil during the mid-60s.

I once went to the neighboring town of Murici about forty-five minutes away by square wheeled bus on dirt roads in the summer. During the rainy season, it was sometimes a two-and-a-half-hour trip when the roads turned into slush and deep mud holes. On several occasions, we all got out to push the bus before getting it going again.

We had to cross several wooden bridges which were more planks than a structure and overturned buses and accidents were frequent. When accidents happened, the bus driver, if he had survived, would quickly disappear into the cane fields never to be seen again.

On this trip to Murici, I stayed with friends Jim and Linda. As they were friends with the owner of the Usina (sugar plantation) they arranged to get three handsome-looking horses with expensive leather saddles. They were shiny new. I don't recall using a step stool to mount my horse, but the ground seemed quite a way away from where I sat.

The last time I ever recalled riding anything resembling a horse was being strapped on to a pony at the county fair and being lead around in a circular wheeled harness. This was different, I wasn't strapped it, my feet didn't reach the stirrups, and all I knew about horses was from old Roy Rogers flics. I prayed that "Giddy up" and "Whoa" was all the vocabulary that I needed.

To be upon such a beautiful animal made one appreciate nature especially under a hot Brazilian sun riding in stringy fields of cane as far as the eye could see. It was a dream.

The dream, however, became a nightmare the next day when I felt something horrendously wrong with my body. Upon trying to sit upon my straw mattress, I was not able to move an inch, not even being able to get out of bed. Every muscle in my body was in involuntary shutdown. Riding for the uninitiated does have consequences and I knew it then and there. All the elasticity in my body had been expended, and I pleaded for the liniment bottle.

That evening, Jim told me this story about his young neighbor that he had befriended. João must have been around 16 years old and had never left his town of 2,000. He proudly told Jim that on the last market day, he had bought a horse, a much-valued commodity. The thing was that João didn't have any money, but was able to persuade the old man to part with the animal. No money exchanged hands, but João did have a cheap, gold-plated ring which had already made his ring finger green and so he somehow did a little horse-trading, a horse for a ring.

The old man told him, "OK, but he no look too good." It didn't matter to João that the horse looked like a bag of bones so he named it Gillette, a common razor blade brand. Brazilians typically did not give pets names of people like Cecelia, my pet donkey.

Young João was delighted and excited. He immediately went into the campo (field) to cut fresh grass for Gillette. He laid it out, but the horse didn't eat anything. Maybe a wrong kind of grass, so João went out the next day for more grass, maybe greener grass, but again, the horse didn't eat anything. It went on for several days until finally, João opened its mouth to force-feed it only to discover that it had no teeth. Not only that, but he soon realized that the horse was also blind.

So here was a situation where a blind, toothless horse was traded for a questionable gold-plated ring that turned your finger green.

The old timer was right, however in saying that his horse didn't look too good."

I'd say it was an even trade unlike conman Jose Cassiano De Jesus, and he was not at all like his namesake, "Jesus."

That's Earle, brother
www.ricetreechronicles.com

Along the Ho Chi Minh Trail

Bullets Cost Too Much

Cambodia still haunts me. I have been there twice in the past year and after years of failed attempts to get into the country, I found myself wanting to get out just as quickly as I had entered.

It is not rational nor explainable. It is just a feeling that I had when I flew to Siem Reap, home to the famous Angor Wat ruins. This ancient site was built around the twelfth century and endured as both a Hindu and eventually a Buddhist religious site. It is the largest temple complex in the world today.

Maybe a hint of what was to become this unshakeable dark feeling was passing by former Cambodian land mine survivors. All with missing limbs, some still dressed in military garb, but still having the heart to play and sing haunting melodies. I remembered little else, not the thick limestone moats surrounding the complex, the massive grounds with temple complexes, libraries and rooms of worship, nor the copious stone etched reliefs of what appeared to be Cambodian dancers in the royal court. I remember the urhu whose bowed strings and melodic sounds pierced the dense jungle canopy and sought out the dark, cool walls of the inner chambers of Angkor Wat.

I left Siem Reap not in awe, contrary to what others have expressed, but with a not too positive feeling about it. So, I asked others who have visited. Most loved Siem Reap, but a few shared similar dark feelings.

Not wanting a negative opinion of any country to be a part of my experience, I crossed the border again by bus a year later. This time, it was at Poipet near the Thai frontier. I sought out the town of Battambang, home to the "Bamboo Train."

My contact there was Sokum, a young Cambodian, maybe all of 22. I spent the entire day on the back seat of his brother's motorbike as we crossed kilometers and kilometers of rice paddies, duck farms and little villages.

Our goal was to ride the "Bamboo Train," a remnant of the French Colonial period. Only the tracks were French; there really was no train, but rather flat, roofless, door-sized railway platforms powered by gas lawnmower engines. Two or three passengers including the motorman could squat comfortably on the open platform, but when met by a similar oncoming vehicle, both would stop and one would decide who was to derail and dismantle their vehicle. Passengers would get off, step to the side while the motorman would disassemble the car removing platform, engine and wheels then let the other pass and reassemble the vehicle to continue on the journey.

The clicky-clackity sounds, made by thumb sized gaps in the snaking rails, broke the silence of the brown, dry, harvested rice fields.

Just before dusk, we headed to the sacred mountain where Sokum wanted me to see the killing fields. It was a mountain top cave attainable by walking up a thousand stairs with a stick in hand, not to support my gimpy knees, but rather to fight off the voracious band of attacking monkeys who have come to expect handouts from visitors.

Eerily peering into the mouth of the giant skull-like cave gave me "chicken skin." Here political prisoners, academics, priests and anyone who did not look Cambodian enough or appeared to be intellectuals were marched up in droves, held prisoner, interrogated and subsequently whacked over the head with a bamboo stick whereupon they fell into the deep pit below. Bullets cost too much. It is said that over ten thousand were summarily executed here.

As dusk approached, we descended as we had come, now to the bottom of the same mountain, but on the opposite side where a crowd had gathered to watch. Like clockwork, millions of bats swarmed out of a small cave undulating in the waning light of the evening sky like a giant Anaconda. They kept coming for almost three quarters of an hour. The hair on the back of my neck stood on end.

The irony was unmistakable. Lives were snuffed out at the top of the mountain and the specter of phantoms flying into the night in the shape of bats fluttered out the other end.

So for me, it was not the reaction to the historical, religious and tourist sights, but rather the stories about what happened to a quarter of the Cambodian people between 1975-1979. This time, the stories came from the dead.

I left Cambodia a second time. I gave it a second chance, but I still left with the same feeling of a country that had shed a lot of tears and blood and whose ghostly spirits still fly the evening skies.

That's Earle, brother
Battambang, Cambodia

Good Bye Mali, Hello Spain

I could tell when I woke up this morning that it was going to be a different day. I mean it isn't everyday that I wake up to a chorus of Gregorian chants from the Benedictine monks of Santo Domingo de Silos at 6:00 AM.

I was in the middle of the Basque Wine country with its rolling hills and endless fields of well-maintained vineyards. Surely, this was a special place.

The chanting, which I could only assume was our wake up call, beat my normal alarm with the song "Abril" by Malpais. On any given day, waking up to it would have started a pleasant day. Waking up to Gregorian chanting was nearly a religious experience when on the Camino de Santiago in an old stone albergue (pilgrim hostel).

The owners of this albergue, the only one in town, knew how to get everyone up with tender care. No sleeping in here. In fact, all "Peregrinos" had to vacate the premises by 8:00 in the morning. It was nothing really difficult as Pilgrims tend to get early starts.

As I walked through the early morning darkness, it was nearly 7 degrees Celsius or about 44 Fahrenheit. When walking though, it didn't feel so cold and the early morning quietness along the vineyards made one wish to be able to preserve that special moment only to realize that it would be impossible. It had to be experienced.

At day break, lo and behold, I saw people actually working in the fields. I had yet to see anyone in the hay fields or vineyards and here they were in plain sight. I decided to go over and talk to them.

It turned out that Sr. Mikel, a common Basque name, and his son were the owners and invited me to take pictures and to talk to his men. I told them that I was from Hawaii and got an "Aloha" from his son as well as a "I am from Hawaii too" from one of the male harvesters. It was comical because from what I could tell, they all appeared to be young African men. I watched and then spoke to the friendliest of the bunch.

"Where are you from?" I asked.

"I am from Mali."

"Wow, you are a long way from home."

"Mali is not so far."

On the map, it didn't appear so, but it must have been a hardship as I did not see any African women working alongside them.

It seemed all too common that immigrants from other countries are ending up doing the jobs that locals do not seem to want. In Thailand, the "I don't want those jobs" are done by the Burmese. In Dubai it's the Filipinos and Indonesians who are the domestics. In the U.S. it's the Guatemalans, Hondurans and Mexicans who work the fields and in other less desirable jobs. In Canada it's the Jamaicans and in Costa Rica, the Nicaraguans are the ones toiling in the banana fields. And in Spain, so are the many young African men from poorer African countries.

I kept wondering who was going to pick all the acres and acres of ripening grapes on the vine. I didn't see young Spaniards in the towns and barrios along the way and the fruits were ripe and ready now, so much so, that I have encountered hundreds of bunches of overripe grapes thrown to the ground to rot.

Sr. Mikel explained, "We are picking the last of the grapes for white wine then it will be time to harvest the grapes for making red wine."

I have presented this question to many Peregrinos. "Have you ever noticed that when you walked though many villages along the Camino, the homes were shuttered and doors closed? I sometimes never saw a soul in many towns. Why was that?"

Some didn't notice. Others speculated. A Canadian told me that an old man was discovered dead in an abandoned building in Cirueños. His family never returned to care for him. One Spaniard told me, "Papi, only the old folks are left in these towns. The young ones have all left as there is nothing here for them. That's why they are shuttered. No one lives in them now. They have moved away. There are few jobs here since the real estate bust in 2008."

But even then, I have noticed similar scenes even in the cities along the French Route of the Camino. Shops were closed more often than they were open and there appeared to be few people shopping. It happens that in Pamplona and Logroño that from around 2:00-5:00, many shops closed for siesta and some didn't even bother to open up at all after that. It seemed common enough to open from 10:00-2:00, then call it a day.

When I did see crowds of people in the larger towns, it was from 6 P.M. on, but they did not appear to be shoppers. They weren't carrying bags or packages. They just seem to be "paseando" or strolling.

I was beginning to wonder how the Spanish economy managed to stay afloat. In contrast, Barcelona seemed to be a different animal. A different work ethic seemed to be driving their economic success. It appeared to be a totally different country to me. Hmmm, maybe peace and quiet was not so bad after all.

And that was what made the majority of the pueblos on the Camino so appealing. The quietness and tranquility of the wine country with its rich sense of history wasn't so bad and the wine was excellent.

That's Earle, brother
Cirueños, Spain
2016

How to Make a Small Fortune in Thailand

Having come from a business family on Maui, I have been fortunate to have had an insider's take on running a business. At best, it is a life where you don't exactly own the business, but where the business owns you. It was difficult then and seemingly getting even harder today, but to the credit of both my grandparents, they did it even when they could barely speak English. It seems that they were made of sterner stuff, not like we third generation privileged book learners. Few from our current generation have taken the plunge into business. I recall quite well my parents' admonition that it takes seven years before your business will even be successful. Yet the appeal of having your own business is there and so my continued interest in being with the business community as well as those who wish to start a business.

Fortunately, I have been blessed with an abundance of experienced human resources. I have had the advantage of having a firsthand look into how to make a small fortune in Thailand and the challenges are unsurprisingly immense.

Cousin Randy has successfully run his own real estate rental business in Bangkok for some 8-10 years. Friend

Dave is completing a masters degree program in international business and Thai friends like Khwan, Tusa and the Wrangler have all had experiences aplenty to share.

It is through these individuals that I based my observations and final conclusions of sort. Research is critical as daughter Nan is still pursuing a lifelong dream of jumping into a food related industry in Chiang Mai, despite completing her degree in nursing. I had advised her early on in high school to pursue her passion and she did just that. It's just that her cooking passion couldn't pay the bills.

Well maybe now, with a steady income, she might still pursue her dream, owning her own food related business however simple it might be.

But let the budding entrepreneurs beware, making a small fortune in any country can have its unique blend of a learning curve through a winding cultural minefield.

Khwan shared this with me. "I was not always a manicurist. I used to sell noodles you know. I could make noodles for 30 cents a bowl and sell for seventy five cents. When the police ask me for bribery money, I tell them how can give you money I no have? But my business not last long, only three months. Cannot make money, but I have to do what I must, not what I want. Even now I thinking of selling noodles out of my house on my day off and delivering them by motorbike. I think some Thai already doing this, but I am thinking of trying. Maybe can make a little money."

"I am lucky because my father doesn't need help. He has a new wife and together they sell food on the street in their town. I live alone so I have to try."

To her credit, Khwan is already saving so she can attend a cosmetology school where she can learn to style both men and women's hair and hopefully open up a complete service shop of her own.

The lure of owning a business is there. The need to prepare for one's future is essential. There is no Social Security net to speak of and so the common bond for many is the very long, difficult road in securing some sort of financial security.

For the last three years that I have known Khwan, she has been the best manicurist in Chiang Mai. I tell everyone that and refer friends and relatives to her whenever I can. She may make her small fortune some day, but for now it is not easy. This afternoon, I was her first customer and it was nearly 1:30.

Tusa is another Thai that I have known for several years and one who ventured out into unknown territory by establishing her own spa. It was something she wanted to do. Unlike with Khwan, it was a choice. She worked at a spa which was the very first that Ms. Carolina and I visited in Chiang Rai years ago. Wanting something more, she, her husband and family borrowed money from friends and family members with the promise to repay them at a later time.

As I had met her husband and knew her father-in-law, I took an interest in their project.

Tusa selected her spa smack dab in the middle of a spa patch; spas were lined up six deep. To me, she had to make her spa stand out or she would quickly go under. In fact, next to her shop, I met several American expats who predicted her shop was no different than most; it would fold in 6 months. They were mistaken. Everyone pitched in to make this venture a success. Tusa's brother Toom was an electrician. Her friend from Bangkok, whose family owned several businesses, loaned her $10,000 as well as from her mother for whom it was a considerable sum.

On that visit, I offered to help furnish the ground floor thinking I knew something about interior decorating. I, as well as her many supporters, was in for a rather rude awakening. The expats' prediction was off by six months. She lasted a year before finally closing her shop amid much angst. She started out bigger than most and fortunately was able to repay her creditors.

"No more. Oh, I don't like. Sometime no money come in. I think better I work for another shop." I guess even with deep pockets, there are no guarantees.

On Soi 11 on Sukumvit Road in Bangkok, I had met the Wrangler, an American businessman. He was a Texan who apparently was in business with his Thai friends. He seemed to have been doing well. I wrote about meeting him several years ago. (See Wrangler in the Catbird Seat). He seemed to be experienced and well connected with his Thai partners who knew how to wind their way through the maze of business regulations and laws that even well heeled foreigners would find challenging.

I still recall his words, *"Well, to be successful here in Thailand, it's who you know and not necessarily what you know. Many businesses fail, but my Thai family is good at what they do. They know the right people."*

However, in the past year or so, I had not seen the Wrangler in his usual seat at his favorite hangout. He prided himself on being served and always had his special table and chair reserved only for him at his restaurant.

The only conclusion that I can draw is that the Wrangler too has been ground to dust and washed away by the monsoon rains. Making a small fortune continues to be tough here in Thailand.

But the one person who seems to have a grasp of the big picture has shared his take on the business scene here and has made sense. Friend Dave has explained the foundation of most businesses here in Thailand. Being a businessman with academic credentials as well as experience, his observation was credible.

"You know Dave, we've spent many an hour discussing and sharing the stories of people we have known and how well their businesses have fared in Thailand."

"Well, I have a theory about that, Papi."

"In the many classes that I have taken here, taught mainly by Thai nationals, I have been privileged to have gained some insight into the business scene in Thailand. Simply put, ... *To make a small fortune in Thailand, one must start with a large fortune.*"

And so, there you are dear readers and future entrepreneurs. Best of luck to you. As for me, I am glad that I went into teaching as a career.

That's Earle, brother
Bangkok, Thailand
2020

A lesson from the Peanut Lady

I like to think that my earliest and best teachers were the women that helped to raise me. I've often spoken of all the things I really needed to know in life, I learned from my grandmother. But along the way, many of us will have had the good fortune of learning from others no matter the circumstance, no matter the country. We are all students or teachers and hopefully with the wisdom of years behind us, we will share what we have learned. As friend Fuku always said, "what good is knowledge if it is not to be shared."

Thus in life, I can claim to have learned a bit and now may be at that stage where I can begin to share what I've learned.

Even something as simple as eating can be a learning as well as a teaching moment. It's not about lessons in nutrition or table etiquette, but rather the discovery that opens up to you during a simple eating experience. In my case, eating out while traveling overseas usually means street food, mom and pop restaurants and sharing food with friends. Each country has their own customs and sometimes surprises.

When I first arrived in an area of Guanacaste, Costa Rica I went to a local restaurant. It was a simple, thatched hut with bamboo lats strung together as table tops. The food must have been good as it was standing room only so I waited in line only to be told..."go sit there, señor, there is an empty chair at that table." Yes, an empty chair with four strangers all eating together.

"Come señor, come sit with us. The food here is good. Muy rico." Uncomfortable at first, it soon dawned on me that this is how dining out should be. Sit at a table with strangers who will soon become friends over the sharing of a meal. It was like that in Hanoi over bowls of hot pho noodle soup. I've made friends with people from all over the world and somehow the food tastes even better in the company of new friends.

On my first visit to Chiang Mai, friend Toom took us to a cultural show replete with a 7-course dinner along with entertainment. We didn't know any better and when the first dish was brought to our table, we dived in head first, no conversation, but inhaling copious amounts of unfamiliar food.

"Wait, wait friends, slow down. Thai people eat very slowly because we serve several dishes at a meal."

It seems we never heard our driver's advice. We were practically full on the first dish. When Thai people eat, it is an experience in the richness of sharing. Duen, one of my former students from Issan would share freshly grown rice from their farm to be eaten in the city with friends and family. Somehow, learning about the cultivation of rice in Thailand and the intensity of manual labor, brings out the richness of its flavor. Meals are experiences because every grain of rice is a labor of love and necessity.

My mom liked to say, don't waste rice, eat every grain of rice and we didn't waste. My Norwegian friend Thore said he tried to help his Thai wife's family by going out into the fields to harvest rice. Even as a young man, he didn't last a day. Just watching the farmers in the rice fields with their backs bent low and up to their knees in water, made him exhausted.

But somehow, in Southeast Asia, I don't see a whole lot of people who are overweight. I've been told more than once that Thai women are attracted to stout men as it would be a sign that they can feed themselves, a sure sign of wealth. True or not, there seems to be fewer bulging waistlines in Thailand.

I've read with some dismay that Westerners are grossly overweight compared to the world population. Yes, with "Big Gulps", triple grilled burgers with layers of bacon and cheese and everything in between and an NFL serving of fries will surely skew the scales to one side.

Like many, I too have had to battle the occasional bulge. It's never easy and no amount of dieting seems to have the lasting and desired effect. There is no sure fire method although I have been given some sound advice in the past.

"Strong arms Papi! You need strong arms to maintain your ideal weight." I asked Frank, "what do you mean, 'strong arms?'" "Well, you've got to be able to push yourself away from the table." It made sense to me.

But the lasting impression that I am still reminded of came by way of a two day "slow boat" ride down the Mekong River on my way to Pak Beng, Laos. The river boat carried mostly foreign tourists, but also local farmers who carried their produce of vegetables, chickens, assorted aquatic animals like frogs and fish to the next village to sell.

On the second day, an old lady with a load larger than herself came on board. The locals all sat on the deck between the tourists. She never said a word, but seemed to be in a peaceful world of her own. As I was gobbling handfuls of shelled roasted peanuts one after the other as though eating was more important that breathing, I offered her some which she graciously accepted. I watched her eat.

Slowly, she'd pop one in her mouth followed with slow and methodical chewing. She seemed to savor each individual nut in slow motion. In the other hand, she held about 5 peanuts which she slowly moved around and around in some kind of circular motion as though counting or massaging them. After a few more minutes, she'd pop another peanut in her mouth. It must have taken her thirty minutes to consume the peanuts, but she seemed to derive much pleasure from this pace.

That image has always stayed with me and when I find myself with handfuls of nuts, jelly beans, cookies and any other type of "finger" food, I pause and remember, then ever so consciously, chew slower and remember the lesson that I learned from the Peanut Lady.

That's Earle, brother
Along the Mekong River
Pak Beng, Laos

A Moment in Time

(The Camino de Santiago is a tributary of interconnecting pilgrim trails that begin in France, England, Ireland, Portugal and Spain and continue on to Santiago de Compostela, in Galicia, Spain. For a thousand years, pilgrims have made the trek, from their countries of origin, mainly on foot and with little possessions. The stories collected along the Camino de Santiago were mainly heard and spoken entirely in Spanish though not always from pilgrims, but from ordinary citizens that were met along the way.)

A moment in time, when two strangers meet can be a special encounter as it may have been for Hilde and the Stranger. It was a Saturday morning under partially cloudy skies when walking down a path to a private beach that a very well-dressed woman with immaculately coiffured hair with a tinge of platinum gray, a pair of designer dark glasses, silk patterned scarf and matching mohair tailored coat and trousers spoke to the stranger while looking towards the beach.

"Do you think we are allowed to walk here?"

The stranger replied confidently, "I think so Señora, as I've seen others walking and jogging along here. I don't think it'll be a problem."

So they continued to walk and occasionally chat. Her name was Hilde and she was a young looking 83 year old. While she did not walk fast, she appeared quite steady on her feet.

He slowed his pace to walk alongside her. She spoke clearly in a very understandable Spanish.

"You know I don't walk fast, but I still enjoy walking and with time, I can eventually get to where I want."

"Yes, walking slow is fine, he said and if we have the time, we can eventually get to where we want to go."

"Hilde, may I ask what you did in your working life?"

"I was a manager in a nice hotel in Menorca, an island in the Mediterranean."

"You know, we are both from islands. I am from the island of Maui, in Hawaii."

"Oh, yes, being in the hotel business we are quite familiar with Hawaii. It's a beautiful place."

The stranger introduced himself. "Me llamo, Papi."

"Oh, that means 'father.'"

"Yes," he replied quickly, "it is an easy enough name to remember, who can say Earle anyway." Still worried a bit, she asked again, "You think it'll be okay that we are here?" Again, he replied with confidence, "Oh, yes Hilde. Besides if anyone questions us, I'll tell them that you are my aunt and that you grew up here as a little girl." That brought a smile to her face.

"I want to ask you something, but I am not sure how to say it in Spanish." In perfect English, she said, "Then say it in English."

Her mannerism gave him a sense of a very well-educated woman.

"Somehow, it seems that this place holds a special meaning for you."

"Actually, my mother grew up here, but it was different then. My father was in the military. But I love the quiet, slow pace of A Coruña. It is a place of pleasant memories."

"Yes, and this stroll appears to be a walk back in time," he added. They both walked a measured pace with moments of conversation mixed in with shared silence.

Before parting, Hilde suggested that he go to Andalusia specifically to Sevilla, Cadiz, Granada and Málaga.

"Son preciosas."

He smiled and thanked her for her recommendations.

When they went their separate ways, he turned to call her and to get a picture of them together, but by then, she was half way up the hill; a lone figure steadily making her way...somewhere.

It was a brief moment in time when two strangers met and their lives intersected. Just as quickly as they met...they parted. However, it left him strangely happy for that encounter. He had engaged a stranger and though they parted as lesser strangers, it was a moment in time that they shared with no one else.

That's Earle, brother
A Coruña,
Galicia, Spain
2022

A New Day for Dagna

(From a Conversation in Spanish)

A dark and cloudy sky forecasted more rain today and there was little hope of enjoying a walk as everyday has been walking in the cold rains of Northwestern Spain. It would be no different this morning and after only 5 minutes the man turned back to the hotel where an equally dismal breakfast awaited him. If another cold breakfast was in the works, it would not be a good day. He had low expectations for the afternoon.

At the waterfront, where the morning fog hung low over the buildings, he walked almost alone with few strangers as companions. What do people do on a rainy Sunday morning," he had asked Simone his cab driver as she dropped him off. "Well, it's Sunday and everything would be closed...shops, cafes, malls, everything. You either stay at home and drink or go out and drink."

Well, it didn't seem like much of an option. Stay in his hotel room and drink or walk in the rain on empty, lonely streets. He opted for the rain swept streets of the harbor.

While looking at all the yachts of various sizes and configurations in the port, a voice from the thick fog reached out to him. Not having noticed anyone next to him, but knowing that it was not his imagination and that the question was clear and distinct, but in a very atypical Iberian accent, he listened intently.

"De donde es ese barco?" The voice was unexpressive, but audible and looking straight ahead, as two strangers might do, he addressed the voice and not the person. "Let's see, that one is from England and the one next to it, is from Norway. There's one from Sweden over there as well as one from France. You can tell by the flags that they fly on their sterns. The flags on their main mast are the host country's flag."

Somehow, he felt he needed to fill in the silence, but the woman seemed genuinely curious about the boats and without barely a glance his way continued. "Are they expensive?"

"Well, some are, if they are new and can easily run half a million Euros, but then you can buy a boat as cheaply as a few thousand Euros, but it may take you years to repair and rebuild if you do the work yourself.

He wasn't a sailor, but attributed his keen sense of yachts through You Tube videos. He realized that he didn't have it in him to sail solo around the world, but allowed himself to fantasize. In his mind, he had already sailed solo from Portugal to England, crossed the Atlantic, sailed through the Panama Canal and on to the Marquesas and New Zealand. He had single handedly reefed sails in "tormentas" in following seas, hauled anchor by hand till his hands bled and scraped the boat's hull under water in Fiji. He scraped and repainted the steel deck of his 37 footer after every long haul when rust started to stain and age his vessel. He drank more than his share of warm Hinano beer along the way.

So it was, armed with this kind of knowledge, that he was able to carry on this early conversation in a Casablanca like fog that lifted quickly.

"What kind of ship is that over there," she asked, pointing to a large gray ship docked away from the other boats. "That's the French warship Alsace, he replied only because he could plainly see the name on the stern. It arrived yesterday." Of course, he only knew that bit as he had seen it approaching land near the Tower of Hercules the day before. That it was French was because of its truck sized stern flag.

After walking a spell, he suggested they have a cup of coffee and so they sat and chatted on a street side cafe and then talked some more. Now looking at the woman for the first time, he asked "Donde eres?"

"You know Señor, I'm actually from Venezuela and I've been here about a year now taking care of my grandfather. My entire family lives in Venezuela and my parents are still there, but President Maduro is a bad man. His military soldiers shot and killed my son who was a second-year medical student protesting peacefully for Democracy. On that day, fifteen people were shot, I knew then that I had to leave, but it wasn't easy. I worked long hours selling fruit and helping my mom to sew clothes. I saved Bolivars, Dollars, whatever I could and had to hide them away or get robbed. But life wasn't always bad in Venezuela. I can remember as a young girl paddling in a dugout canoe and arriving in Manaus, Brasil. My father made and sold drums out of native trees and played for a traveling 'Capoeira' show."

"You may have read how difficult it is for Venezuelans under Maduro. We had no food. Lines were blocks long just to get toilet paper and some rice and our money was worth nothing; it changed in value from day to day. The equivalent of a hundred dollars would last only 5 days in Venezuela but that amount can sustain us for 15 days here in Spain. Now, with the pandemic in Venezuela, people are dying left and right. In the past two months, four in my family died of Covid 19. Fortunately, I was able to get the vaccine here, but that is not really feasible back home where many in my family are trapped and are no longer able to leave the country."

"I remember clearly trembling as I walked across the border to freedom a few years ago. My breaths were quick, shallow and deliberate; my legs were shaking as I crossed the Simon Bolivar Bridge, a mere several hundred meters separated us from the Venezuelan end to the other side in Columbia. The border guards asked me if I was planning to live in Columbia, but I said, 'No sir, I will move on.' That's when they stamped my passport and said, 'Welcome to Columbia!' I was so happy I could only kiss the ground."

"After reaching Bogota, I kept moving on, going next to Peru and Brasil then eventually to Spain. I guess that's why I like boats. It might take me to a place where I'll be happy and safe."

"And so, you are here in Spain," he replied with his eyes smiling.

"Yes, were it not for family, I would still be a nomad adrift from place to place."

"Well, you haven't lost your Latin American accent and that was the only reason I could understand you so well..." They both laughed and continued sip their coffee for an hour till the cold winds from the Atlantic chilled their cafe con leche which then became undrinkable.

They continued to walk and chat and only in parting, did she finally say, "My name Dagna."

Curious about her name which was unusual, he later discovered that it meant "a new day."

Hopefully for Dagna, it would also mean a new start in life.

That's Earle, brother
Somewhere in Spain
2022

She Danced the Night Away

Salon Getsemani with its 39 foot curving laminated wood bar with torn vynil stools stood empty, but all was not silent. The blaring sound track inside the bar blotted out the afternoon traffic, but for some reason, I was the only patron in what I would have expected would be another popular spot on calle Larga, a two lane, one way street that serves as a speed way early in the mornings.

A single masked worker stood patiently by one of the two double front doors, although looking for customers, she was not calling out to anyone. Obviously bored, she paced from door to door. Her hands clasped behind her back, she appeared to not notice the afternoon traffic with honking horns and speeding motor bikes. It was a typical day in this part of Getsamani.

It has been a hour since my arrival and across the street the Centro Comercial has already closed its doors early for another night of revelry in the city of Cartagena.

If the previous night was any indication, the partying was joyfully attended by families as well as young singles and couples. Earlier, the hotel desk clerk had said, "Senor, everyone will party late into the night and the streets will be crowded for sure then tomorrow everything will be closed.

Too much drinking." He was right. Later that evening, one would barely be able to walk the same streets which only the night before seemed rather sedate, but was now transformed into a standing room crowd with occasional cars honking their way patiently through the crowds waiting for an opening.

Entertainers were aplenty. A conga dance group of about 20 dancers and musicians planted themselves on the small square fronting the church while performers shimmied to the beat of several drums, gourds and a single high pitched wood flute. As the volume rose, the atmosphere was heightened by the blurring motions of the dance troupe all dressed in native costumes with the men carrying torches.

A young saxophonist tried unsuccessfully to inch his way into a spot on the asphalt for the next spot. The African dancers and drummers would be a hard act to follow and there was no opening for him so he moved on unnoticed. No sooner did the troupe pack up and leave then in a split second on walked what appeared to be an obviously very pregnant and barefooted lady with a light coffee colored complexion who seemed bent on securing a spot to perform.

A flat, mini bikini top revealed a stomach the size of a giant brown turtle shell and behind her halter and her black feather skirt a large triangular like kerchief hugged her hips which was adorned with sequins and rhinestones and with dangling threads of silver tassels with colored beads. The crowd, estimated to be nearly several thousand strong had now huddled into the small square and turned their attention to the numerous food vendors circling the edges of the street like covered wagons in a western. A threesome of young foreigners maintained their front seat status at a sidewalk cafe fronting center stage and continue to sip their cold beers heavy with condensation. They had an unobstructed view.

Much of the crowd initially did not seem to take notice of the young lady, who by this time had placed her portable speaker nearby and adjusted the volume before suddenly jumping up and down, shifting her weight from the ball of one foot to the other and shaking her unveiled pregnant features disregarding a possible miscarriage. Each motion, every move and turn made the glitter and tassels take flight like a bumblebee to the thumping and mesmerizing sound track. Her belly moved like an undulating psychedelic snake digesting its prey as her stomach moved in and out in rhythmic motion. Her gyrations created waves of vibrations that reverberated through the crowd, suddenly electrifying them and all eyes were upon her at center stage. The foreigners put down their beers. The young lady mouths the voice over, pouts and blows kisses to the audience with every part of her pliant and supple body supporting her moves. People clapped to the beat. The woman is encouraged and stops gyrating between pauses in the sound track, feigns another pout, a finger pointing to a dimple, followed by a kiss and continued to quiver again at an even more feverish pace.

It is amazing what the human body can do and it is quite apparent that the performer is skilled at the art of flexibility and with a well-rehearsed routine in mind. The crowd swoons and sways in unison. They are now one.

It was a demonstration of stage presence where the previous act of prominent dancers and drummers were now a long-forgotten memory. The crowd shouted for more and the performer delivers.

Cars crammed their way past the crowds, albeit moving slower to get a glimpse of the one woman show stopper. Food vendor sales stall with the performance as the vendors themselves stretched over others to get a glimpse. Customers stand in awe ignoring their food in hand which starts to cool.

The undulations continued with a crescendo reminiscent of Ravel's Bolero, building and winding to a heightened pitch as both dancer and music now reached the imaginary peak with the crowd holding their breath. The thrilling end reaches its climax and suddenly crashes in blinding speed.

The gathering is drenched in sweat brought on by the dancer as well as the evening's humid weather. For those at a distance, the end comes too quickly, but they clamor for more; Some remain motionless and others somehow expecting more. However, the music's finale signaled the end of the synchronized combination of bumps and grinds as she brings both out stretched hands in front her into a sign of peace and thanks.

The pregnant young performer slowly and deliberately waltzes over to the young threesome with the grace of a prima ballerina in bare feet and does a low bow. The men clap enthusiastically, even rising to the occasion. Although appearing puzzled at first, they break out in smiles as they realize, upon closer inspection that the very pregnant young lady was not quite with child, but a supple young feminine looking man, with rubio colored hair and a fetching, but beguiling smile. His delicate and expressive facial features with a sumo sized belly fooled many.

A dozen street cleaners, in single file, wearing yellow reflective jump suits with matching hats and pushing their carts signaled the final curtain call; their work day was just beginning, but the festivities continued.

That's Earle, brother
Getsamani, Cartagena
Colombia
2022

Sizzler and the Amazing Angels

I have been blessed on many of my travels with wonderful people who have opened their homes and hearts to me, with exciting little adventures in far off exotic locations and with the occasional exceptional days unlike many others.

Today was such a day. I was on my way to meet cousin Randy and a few friends for a quiet lunch. What could be better than that?

While walking to Ekamai station on the Sukhumvit line was an option, I was much too far away at the other end of town. I couldn't possibly walk the four miles in time for lunch, but at least I would try.

Another hot, humid day in Bangkok and walking would be taxing, but I attempted it. About half way to my destination, I realized that the rest of the way would just take too long; the buffet line would be overflowing. It was best to take the BTS Skytrain in cool air-conditioned comfort for only 28 baht, less than a dollar.

Getting anywhere in metropolitan Bangkok is best done using public rail transportation. You can get to most places at little expense and ride comfortably. Once at your destination, it would be a simple matter of walking the rest of the way or taking a motorbike taxi to your final destination.

So, it was to be a routine ride. Walk to the upper platform, get change in coins, punch in the correct amount to your destination, insert coins and there it is. Simple.

As I entered the mildly crowded car, two of the most gorgeous young ladies sat not more than ten feet away from me. I could not help, but stare. Somehow, they were grossly out of place. Elegantly dressed with nothing less than peek-a-boo Versace blouses with long, creamy silk pants and diamond studded earrings. Their stature suggested that they were professional models.

I looked around, but saw nothing unusual. I somehow expected cameras to be rolling…they were gorgeous, or did I already say that? They were so stunning that surely they were messengers from heaven.

The Thais are known for their beauty and fashion magazines are full of beautiful people, but this pair would possibly put most of them on some obscure back page; they were that stunning.

It's the kind of situation where you would ask yourself, "Should I take their picture?" I knew that I would never see them again and in all the years of travel, have never personally witnessed such examples of loveliness. It's the kind of situation where, if you don't act, you would regret it the rest of your life. It's the kind of experience that you would revisit time and time again rehearsing what you would have said had you had the charisma and confidence of a James Bond. Somehow, in the movies, they always get it right, but in real life there are no retakes.

I waited. I paused. I considered. I've been told that some of the most beautiful ladies in Bangkok are really not women at all, but men who have chosen to be "ladyboys." In short, Thailand's third sexual gender.

They are often statuesque, bosomy, skimpily dressed and well, exotic looking.

When we first visited Bangkok, Ms. Carolina and I went to the Calypso Club at a nearby hotel. It was reminiscent of Finocchio's in San Francisco where my parents attended a similar cabaret show with a cast made up entirely of men dressed as women. I remembered well. I was about 12 and a twelve year old never forgets photographs of skimpily dressed, exotic looking women.

The Calypso Club was a showcase for Thailand's famous ladyboys. The show lasted 75 minutes and was nonstop showmanship besting anything we have ever seen in Vegas. I was mesmerized. We were mesmerized.

How could men be that gorgeous?

Well, the thought raced through my mind on that short ride. Did they have any traces of an Adam's Apples? No. Did they have manly looking hands? No. What about muscular shoulders? Soft and slender as far as I could see. No, they were 100% female. I am 97% sure.

The train slowed to a stop. All that had happened, took mere seconds and felt like a dream. THEY were getting off! No wait! This isn't my stop! My angels were waltzing out of my life never to be seen again. I must decide now or never.

Do I get off here or continue on to the next stop to my original destination. The passengers were like me. We were frozen with indecision, but we continued to stare as the gorgeous pair, still looking like they didn't perspire like ordinary people and should have been riding in chauffeur driven Bentleys. They were floating out of the car, their feet barely kissing the ground.

Quick, take a picture, stupid! Strange, but everything seemed a blur in slow motion and while they began their egress, the rest of us were frozen in our tracks. I guess, time did stop for that beautiful pair. I was witness to that.

My decision came in a split second, I think. It was walk out with the pair of fashion models a la movie stars or continue to my next stop. A tough decision, but I did decide. I could walk along with the angels for a few mortal and excruciating seconds or meet cousin Randy and friends at the restaurant. What would you have done?

The decision was easy. Boy was that salad bar at Sizzler's amazing.

That's Earle, brother
Bangkok, Thailand

Thank You Josef Korzeniowski

Bangkok in 1888 must have been even more exotic and strange than what it might appear to the typical visitor of today. Surprisingly they did have traffic problems then but mainly where the newly introduced rickshaws created confusion with occasional herds of parading elephants and Ford model T's with untrained drivers who often drove straight into the traffic cops kiosk in the middle of "New Road" in China Town.

On Sampeng Road, in the Gem Quarter, barefooted patrons, children and adults walked shirtless in the streets which then was surprisingly void of motorized vehicles and foreign visitors.

When Teodor Korzeniowski first came to Bangkok as a newly employed sea captain of a derelict ship with a sick crew, many of whom were hospitalized in Bangkok, he anchored his ship near the Oriental Hotel and created a rusting eyesore so much so that occasional comments were made by hotel guests about its embarrassing presence on the Chao Phraya River.

When reading some of Korzeniowski's accounts, I was intrigued and wished to have gotten a glimpse of Bangkok life then. Josef's note taking and keen observation served him well years later when he wrote about his time in Bangkok. It was not in his native Polish, but his stories written in English introduced the world to Bangkok during the late 1800's.

That I love Bangkok is no secret and that I have visited the sights along the Chao Phraya River in hopes of uncovering hidden stories in the narrow "sois" of the city. I always knew that I would one day make it to Thailand, known then more as the Kingdom of Siam on old world maps. There was always an attraction but it was unexplainable nor was it pressing for me to go there; I simply knew that one day, I would go.

As a youngster growing up on Maui, our main contact with the outside world was through the movies and weekly newsreels at one of three movies theaters in town. Of the three, the largest and most modern, only Iao Theater remains in all its glory having been restored a few years ago.

Newsreels, the precursor to television news was typically black and white and came dramatically on screen with a booming narrator's voice. Nothing to recall there, but it seems that the pace of a once a week newscast was sufficient for my taste

The movies, however, were another matter when CinemaScope and the musicals of Rodgers and Hammerstein came out with such blockbusters as the King and I based on the life of an English governess to the King of Siam, King Mongkut, King Rama IV in the 1860's. This glorified musical with elaborate costumes in gold, exotic and spellbinding settings against the background of that period made for riveted viewing.

I believe that it was the right moment in my life whereas a year earlier, I was not quite ready for Oklahoma with so much singing and dancing that an adolescent could barely see beyond his covered face. I can recall my reaction, "Oh brother, not another song." But that was then and when the King and I burst on the big screen, which wasn't so big compared to today, I embraced both music and dance and the only King for me was Yul Brynner with his brilliant and handsome domed head with his regal stance with legs spread apart and hands on his hips. It was my impression that that was the way a King should look.

While the fantasy of the Kingdom of Siam drew me eventually to Thailand, the reality was a bit more sobering. Still, there are a lot of glitter and gold left in the many "Wats" and Royal Palaces of Thailand though I have yet to see any royalty sporting that classic stance ala Yul Brynner.

But the draw to old Siam is still there as well as the mysteries of this, at times, puzzling culture. Teodor Korzeniowski acknowledged the Kingdom of Siam and it was he to whom many credit as having introduced Siam to the world.

He often wrote from the grounds of the Oriental Hotel more recognized today as the Mandarin Oriental Hotel and it was an association enough for me to seek out this place and to walk in his footsteps even though I have only read a few of his stories. Like he, however, I could not afford to stay at the Oriental Hotel nor to eat there regularly, but I could at least sit in the writer's lounge which was visited by the likes of Somerset Maugham, James Michener, and Graham Greene and to use their facilities and sip a mint julep and think back to a time when the Kingdom of Siam was not a glossy Hollywood production, but a place where writers went for inspiration. It felt good to at least share the company of famous writers of the past who had strolled through the doors of the Mandarin Oriental Hotel in Bangkok.

Thank you, Teodor Josef Korzeniowski. We know you today as Joseph Conrad. Thank you for bringing us Siam in a purer form.

That's Earle, brother
Bangkok, Thailand

The Man with Sunburnt Legs

El Camino del Norte is a historical Camino that began near the French-Spanish border and runs along the Atlantic Coast until Galicia, Spain and to the final destination of Santiago de Compostela. Often, the pilgrims would continue on to Muxia and Finisterre, then known as the "End of the World" in Medieval times. It was and still is, a popular although challenging Camino through much of northern Spain.

Call it destiny or just plain luck, but I met my first Peregrino (pilgrim) when we lined up together for the Pilgrims mass at Santiago de Compostela. It had been a long week without meeting anyone of consequence and it was beginning to look like a trip of disappointments.

It's unusual that I don't meet people who share their stories with me, but just starting up conversations in pandemic weary Spain was not made any easier with the mandatory use of masks indoors and out. It may have been the masks or the social distancing that were inhibitors to talking or just the environment of larger cities.

I first noticed the young man not because of his tell tale backpack, which seemed rather small and light for a

Peregrino, but because of his sun burnt legs which reminded me of the tourists back on Maui who had been out in the sun way too long. His legs were red and peeling and I thought it rather strange when Galicia had been experiencing overcast days of solid and continual rain. Surely this Peregrino had a story somehow associated with his sunburnt legs.

I spoke first. "Hola Peregrino! Como estas, amigo? Ja completo el Camino?"

"Si amigo, he completado el Camino del Norte en 30 días."

"30 Dias? Dios mío! No caminaba, estaba volando."

We laughed then somehow instinctively switched into English. "Yes, I was walking 25-30 kilometers a day. I love to walk. Since I don't really play any sports, walking is my passion."

"Where are you from my friend?" Which is a standard question all Peregrinos ask each other.

"I'm Viljem from Slovenia. And you are the first person I've spoken to in English. Most people I met didn't speak any English, so this is quite a treat."

"Well, I feel the same way too. I haven't met a friendly face in a week. You are the first, so I am quite happy."

Prevented from entering the cathedral because of limited seating, we opted to sit and chat a bit over a beer which was kept cold with the inclement and cool weather.

"You know Viljem, your pack looks kinda light."

"It's only 7 kilos. I just threw out a bunch of stuff as I walked along the Camino del Norte...didn't need this, didn't need that. You know after a while, my pack got lighter. I just kept a note pad to write things down and I haven't bought anything yet. I just keep everything in here," pointing to his head.

"Ha, we both seem to travel in similar ways, I said. Less is more. I dumped stuff along the way on my Camino. It made for better walking days. In fact, I think I'll mail some clothes home tomorrow. My practice is if I buy something, then I have to get rid of something. Guess I'll have to get rid of several somethings tomorrow."

We both nodded and laughed. Yes, we agreed that we don't need much when we travel and it reminded me of a guy that I met in the Houston airport who after traveling several months in Latin America returned with just a very small, hand-held kitchen sized garbage bag, kinda extreme but he was always a reminder to travel with less. Besides, I've always found that when traveling as a minimalist, you can always buy anything that you need along the way no matter where the country or the circumstance.

Viljem offered this sage advice, "Papi, Given the time, we are capable of walking anywhere."

"I agree Viljem, except that I have less time in front me than behind me, so I like to keep on moving," I said with a wink. "But you know, I don't see a sleeping bag or tent on your pack and Galicia is twenty degrees cooler than Madrid."

"I've slept out mostly in the woods, but I have never been afraid." But when he showed me his set up, I was a bit unprepared. He had just completed 830 kilometers and now the temperature went as low as 59 degrees in rainy Galicia, but he braved the elements and slept outdoors only opting for a hostel every third or fourth night.

"Just to wash up, you know."

So it was not surprising that he walked where he did and was as self-sufficient as he was.

As for his sun burnt legs, well, that came during the walk to the sea at Muxia and Finisterre maybe the only place in all of Galicia at this time to have sunshine.

I invited Viljem to come visit me. Yes, at this rate, I would not be surprised to see him camped out under my lime tree in the backyard. That would be OK. Camping out on Maui would be a lot easier except he'll probably get more sun burnt than just his legs.

You are welcome my friend.

That's Earle, brother
Santiago de Compostela
Galicia, Spain

The Story of Isaias:
I Have to do Something

I remember very little of that day other than it was chilly in the morning and the fog hung low on the mountain. Usually grandma had a fire going by this time of the day, but the house was still cold and very quiet. The smell of wood burning would usually wake me up, but I did not smell any and wanted to sleep a few minutes longer. It was past the peak coffee harvesting season of November and December; the nights were getting colder and the rains would soon be upon us.

There were only three of us now, grandmother and my brother Alexander who was two years younger than me. Our mother died the day Alex was born. I was 2 years old or thereabouts. I don't know what day or year I was born, but I think grandmother would know. She took care of us now that mother was gone and many years earlier my father walked out of the house when mother was pregnant and left with another village woman. They never returned to our community. I think he just went through the door...gone, just like that. I never saw him again and I do not know if I would recognize him.

I have some memory of my mother. Grandmother said she was a strong woman who picked coffee during the peak season, chopped firewood to sell in town and raised a garden of maize, fruits and beans. We didn't raise chickens. They just ran around and we would fetch the eggs and eat them.

There never was much to eat, but I think we had enough although I may never know. One meal a day was usually what we had, but I don't ever remember any particular meal. I know that at a young age, I always drank coffee for breakfast and why not, coffee trees were everywhere and we lived on the side of the mountain where they always grew.

Grandmother would make us coffee and care for the house, prepare meals, wash clothes for us and go into the fields to work. Without a father and mother, grandmother did everything, but I never heard her complain. It was the only life I knew.

Almost daily grandmother would chop wood by going up into the mountains and carrying down a bundle for cooking and heating our one room adobe house. Fortunately, we had a tin roof so much of the rain never entered our house, but with open windows, it was always cold and in the early years I never had any shoes; my feet were always wet and cold.

And so it was strange that I did not awaken to the smell of smoke in the house. It was raining steadily outside. I remember that. There was a moist chill in the air, but no roosters were crowing. Our cat with no name lay near me without making a sound. It usually slept next to me.

When I finally got up, Grandmother was not near the wood burning stove, but I could see her lying still on the bare wooden bed with a thinly woven mat over her. I called, but she didn't answer. "Grandmother, grandmother, wake up...the house is cold." There was no fire, but grandmother lay still and cold as a mountain stone.

Grandmother just lay there. It kept raining. I think I realized that somehow grandmother had gone away, maybe just her spirit, but she was no longer with us. Now we were two, my brother Alexander and I; he was 5 and I was 7.

I didn't cry. I don't know what I felt, but I just knew that I had to do something for grandmother so I went outside to chop firewood as she had done. I chopped for several hours until I had enough of a load that I could sell in the city.

I walked that five miles down the mountain and looked for someone to buy my firewood.

A young American girl saw me walking with my load of firewood and wanted to know why I was selling firewood in the rain. I did not understand her language, but I spoke to the girl next to her who was from town.

"She wants to know why you are walking in the rain with this heavy load of firewood?" I could only cry and tasted my tears along with the rain. I replied, "My grandmother died this morning. I have to do something."

That's Earle, brother
In the coffee fields above Copan Ruinas
Thanksgiving Day
Honduras
2022

Post Script:

I picked coffee with Isaias today, a gentle man of 26 though he looked much older than his years. Remarkably, he raised Alexander by himself and somehow kept them both fed. He washed clothes and knew how to make tortillas out of maize. He never spent a day in school, but was able to get his brother educated for three years. He can neither read nor write, but a more humble man is not to be found.

Today, he has two children, an infant and a child of 9. As a result of this chance encounter with the American gal some 19 years ago as a child of 7 carrying a load of firewood to sell in the rain there may be some help available to him, As he said to me, "I will only ask for help in an emergency."

I have become a fan of Isaias who has had to deal with a lifetime of adversity of which I have only covered one aspect. There may be another chapter to Isaiah's story; it deserves to be told.

I Swear It Was Picasso

It may be my imagination, but I swear that I have seen Pablo Picasso in the streets of Málaga, Spain practically at every corner. The however, is that while I can swear that it was Picasso with his characteristic blue and white striped shirt, he couldn't possibly be at everywhere in the city, nor at the beaches or at a Starbucks sipping one of their terrible cups of coffee.

Maybe it's a promotional by the City fathers to attract more visitors to Málaga now that the flood gates of European cities have let loose the hordes of Covid weary citizens who have had nothing to do, but to save their Euros for a time like this.

And there is no time like now, as Málaga resembles a prepandemic business as usual place, except for the masks. Young parents are seen pushing baby carts under the shade in the city center, chubby little kids run from store front to store front, their ice cream cones melting as fast as they run, friends sip iced latte's on sidewalk cafes, people walk their pet Terriers and crazy young and not so young tourists try eScooters for the first time.

It is almost frightening to see that most of the scooter renters are first timers whose last experience on a scooter was in their childhood. Here, I trusted them to steer clear of me when sharing the same paseo (pedestrian walk way), but having tried it myself, I now realize that they were never in full control of this battering ram. It is a projectile on two wheels, that can reach speeds of up to 20 mph. I know, I tried it and it can be frightening for the inexperienced rider and certainly deadly for the unwary pedestrians.

The single brake on it is questionable at best and there are no instructions or even adverts about insurance should the rider succumb to stationary lamp posts or slow moving pedestrians. What to do? Well, if memory serves me right, keep on trucking and pray for a safe return.

The motor and GPS system work in tandem and should you cross into a "no go" zone, the motor will quit on you and you would be left to your own motor skills to get you back into friendly territory. Yes, I've gone into more than one forbidden area, but was able to walk out safely without a citation to my name.

Still, the lure of an eScooter is mesmerizing even for a septuagenarian. Even old moths are attracted to open flames and those that have survived with only singed wings may still want to try it again. I think I do.

It is all in a day's mix of eBikes which are mere child's play next to eScooters, the likes of which I have never experienced before, but having safely done so may never want to try again.

Maybe that's why I don't like Vegas. I am not a gambler and surely riding an eScooter is far riskier than flying to Vegas for 5 days, at least you don't have to wear a helmet in Vegas.

So I have had my thrills for this day, well, maybe for the rest of my days, but knowing the thrill of the wind blowing in your face leaves one wanting more. Now I understand why dogs stick their heads out of car windows. Tomorrow is another day and should there be more eScooters in my path, I may surely have to think hard and fast about getting aboard one again.

However, I am quite sure that this too shall pass and I will again find comfort and relaxation on the sofa at home, but I swear, I really did see Picasso on an eScooter in Málaga.

That's Earle, brother
On an eScooter
Málaga, Spain
2022

It Happened One Night
In Bangkok

Friends who have been to Thailand and of course to Bangkok seem to be able to take it in small doses for a few days at most, then often head north to Chiang Mai or south to one of several small and popular islands.

Well for me, being an island boy most of my life, there is little appeal in seeing another sandy beach or more sandy beach buns. I rather like city life for a change of pace and a city of 9 million fits the bill for me.

Walking on the streets of Maui while quiet, peaceful and safe, is well, boring. I don't mean the safety part, as I appreciate that aspect of walking at the wee hours of the morning without fear for one's safety. But I never see anyone on the streets. I guess if I did encounter a stranger alone at night I would probably cross to the other side. So it seems somewhat strange that I don't fear for my safety among tens of thousands on the streets on Bangkok all of whom are strangers.

Therein lies the appeal. One sees everything from beggars, tourists in tank tops and flip flops, office girls heading places, freelance hookers and ladyboys, street vendors selling fake everything. They were selling poorly made fake Rolexes, but nothing like the "quality fakes" that I buy. Want a Panerai? They have them too.

What about elephant pants which I am certain more than one person has exclaimed when opening up their suitcase after their Thai holiday and saying, "Good grief, what was I thinking?"

There are street cleaners oddly pushing their broom ahead of them rather than sweeping alongside them, Everyone is going somewhere and where they say that New York is a city that never sleeps, Bangkok seems to be a city drunk on Red Bull. Traffic is always crowded. There are taxi and motor bike drivers aplenty reving their engines and so are the diesel, carbon spewing buses or super-efficient sky train that takes you practically everywhere.

Whistle blowing private traffic security are irritatingly at every driveway blowing their brains out. But against all of this enthusiastic backdrop there are sometimes even more interesting encounters.

Those of us who are comfortable in our situations may find life just fine, but I sometimes get bored on Maui and get a desire to head somewhere. I guess many places would do, but Bangkok has always served up a smorgasbord of characters at any hour and has never disappointed me.

Take last night for example. Before turning in for the night and rounding a corner near my hotel, I noticed another brand new massage spa. It was so new that the wrappings were still on the easy chairs. It looked like a good place to get a foot massaged so I made my way through the glass doors and plopped myself in a chair and prepared for an hour of holy bliss. Just when it seemed like it would be a typical massage, I noticed someone out of the corner of my eye. Not just anyone, but yes, without a doubt, I was convinced that it was Elvis. He was alive and well and uuuh finishing up a foot massage. I couldn't resist and unwrapped my toweled feet and hobbled over to him.

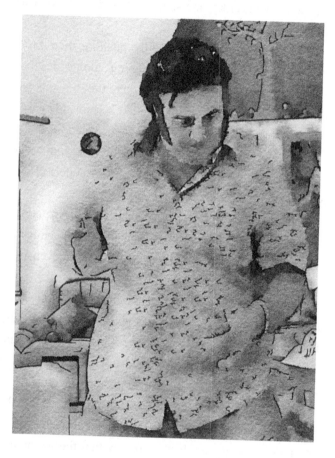

"Excuse me sir. Mr. Presley, I presume?" I was embarrassed, but he just smiled like I always remembered him in Blue Hawaii. "Thank you, Thank you very much." He even sounded like him, then I walked away.

A couple of minutes later, he returned, looked at me straight in the eyes like a hound dog and sang to a capacity crowd of people getting foot massages.

"Well, it's one for the money
Two for the show
Three to get ready
Now go, cat, go
But don't you
Step on my Blue Suede shoes
Wop, wop...wop...wop"

Everyone clapped and we bumped fists. In parting, he said to all, "Thank you, Thank you very much." As he was leaving the spa, I yelled out in my best baritone announcer voice..."Elvis is now leaving the spa."

That's Earle, brother
Bangkok, Thailand
2020

Lucrecia in the Sky with Coffee

High in the mountains above Copan Ruinas where the air is pure and the coffee grows to enormous size, a small community of Hondureno coffee farmers live in near isolation from the town several thousand feet below. Down in the valley, the smoke from burning fields and smog from every kind of vehicle sit on the town like a heavy blanket.

Occasional bareback riders on horse pass us on the narrow winding road towards the top. They usually carry a load of firewood or produce while families walk up the mountain or do a combination of ride and walk; an occasional tuk tuk or two happily head downhill after dropping off passengers and cargo.

The higher we ascend, the greener and thicker the vegetation gets, but no homes are in sight. The dirt road is hard packed and rutted, however still passable during this time of the year while winter rains bring challenges even to well-treaded four-wheel drives.

As we gain altitude above the clouds, the fresher we feel in body and spirit. The view is spectacular in its presentation of the surrounding mountains in this last southern bastion of Mayan culture. It is a view that I have always seen from the city, but never from the vantage point of being at the top of the highest mountain in Copan Ruinas.

From there, we descend slightly into a valley where we meet Isaias (The Story of Isaias) and his kin. They are local coffee harvesters and live in a cluster of small adobe homes. Everyone picks coffee; mothers, fathers, uncles, aunts and neighbors work alongside each other. Children of all ages work with their parents; it is serious work and they get paid for it depending on the amount of beans they pick. The season is brief, but the days are long.

Our driver, Tulio said he used to work in these fields and would pick 8 gallons of coffee a day, quite a considerable sum. "It was hard work, but I enjoyed it and of course I love coffee."

While having a few coffee trees in my back yard does not constitute a farm, the sight of a heavily laden branch of ripe red Arabica does elicit awe. I seldom give thought to how a coffee bean is harvested; only its origin and flavor, but seeing the effort that goes into the harvesting season and the harshness of the conditions give pause to appreciate the beans even more.

Forget the commercialization of Colombian coffee icon Juan Valdez, Isaias and his coffee picking family are the real deal campesinos. They have lived on the mountain side for generations in the same adobe huts as their parents and their parents before them.

The need for masks are redundant here. The fresh air can be filtered no more than can be found in the purest of areas. It is here that families of coffee farmers spend 2 short months during November and December "cortando" (picking) coffee from trees heavily laden with large ripe beans of various shades of red and green. Children as young as 9, and 70-year-old grandmothers pick coffee alongside each other. As it is vacation for the kids, many work alongside their families picking coffee nimbly with their tiny fingers.

Initially, traces of the harvesters are only indicated by the plastic soda bottles of water and lunch sacks hanging from low branches along the road side. Upon closer look, deep and further in, there is movement and some color. A family of workers are here as they fan out in all directions. It is quiet and there isn't much banter going on; surely a sign of serious business.

Beyond the coffee harvesters, we approached an adobe hut hidden by more coffee trees, but overlooking a lumpy, but reasonably flat community soccer field. "You must meet Dona Lucrecia Senor Eraldo, she is a fixture here, but she is down in the valley picking coffee." Somehow, fifteen minutes later, word has reached her and breathing heavily, greets us at her home.

"Welcome to my home...welcome everyone! This is my home." Her smile and enthusiasm spoke volumes. She apparently ran up the hill and at age 70 seemed much more capable than the three of us city dwellers, one of whom was 30 years her junior and using a walking stick.

"Yes," Tulio said, "You need 4-wheel drive here, but our friend Yarely here only has '3 wheels,'" referring to the young gal leaning on her stick. It brought a laugh from all of us.

Quickly gaining her composure, we soon learn that Dona Lucrecia was actually the local potter, well, the only one for that matter. "I learned to make pottery at the age of

9 by watching my mother. I have been doing this for 61 years. I made my own kiln, chop wood, and fire my pieces. This table is where I make my pottery. Occasionally, a customer will come."

Today, according to Tulio, will surely be a good day for Dona Lucrecia.

She is lively, animated and full of energy, the kind of person you would want to share a cup of coffee with and that is what she did. "This is coffee from my yard. Please, please enjoy a cup with me." It was an excellent brew and made even more special because the mugs of coffee were sculptured by her clay-stained hands.

"Dona Lucrecia, while I have no room in my bag, I will still buy a few pieces of pottery from you so that when I drink my morning coffee on Maui, it will bring me back here; up high in the sky drinking coffee with you."

I picked up a shorn horse shoe in front of her house and showed it to Dona Lucrecia. "Senor Eraldo, you must take that with you, then you will remember me and this place." We feigned a wrestling match over the horseshoe. Were it real, she would have surely won. With a smile we bid each other adieu.

"I will come visit you again in another year or two." "Si, senor Eraldo. I will be here and we shall again drink coffee together at my home."

"Yes, Dona Lucrecia, I think that would be a very nice plan."

That's Earle, brother
Copan Ruinas, Honduras
Thanksgiving Day, 2022

Made in the USA
Middletown, DE
11 April 2024

52881999R00106